BUSINESS
WITHOUT
BOSSES

Other Books by Charles C. Manz and Henry P. Sims, Jr.

Superleadership: Leading Others to Lead Themselves
Charles C. Manz and Henry P. Sims, Jr.

The Art of Self-Leadership
Charles C. Manz

Mastering Self-Leadership
Charles C. Manz

Self-Leadership: A Skill Building Series
Charles C. Manz

The New Leadership Paradigm: Social Learning and Cognition
in Organizations
Henry P. Sims, Jr., and Peter Lorenzi

The Thinking Organization: Dynamics of Organizational Social
Cognition
Henry P. Sims, Jr., and Dennis A. Gioia

BUSINESS WITHOUT BOSSES

How Self-Managing Teams Are Building High-Performing Companies

CHARLES C. MANZ

HENRY P. SIMS, JR.

JOHN WILEY & SONS, INC.

New York • Chichester • Brisbane • Toronto • Singapore

This text is printed on acid-free paper.

Library of Congress Cataloging-in-Publication Data:

Manz, Charles C.
    Business without bosses: how self-managing teams are building
  high-performing companies / Charles C. Manz, Henry P. Sims, Jr.
        p.   cm.
    Includes index.
    ISBN 0-471-57700-6 (cloth: acid-free paper)   0-471-12725-6 (paper)
    1. Work groups.   2. Management—Employee participation.
  3. Employee motivation.   4. Industrial productivity.   I. Sims,
  Henry P., 1939–   .   II. Title.
  HD66.M363   1993
  658.4'02—dc20   93-7864

Printed in the United States of America

10 9 8 7 6 5 4 3

To our families:
Karen, Chris, and Katy,
Laurie, Jonathan, Amy, and Andrew—
our favorite SuperTeams

Preface to the Paperback Edition

Popular movements in management theory follow an all too familiar cycle. First, there is the quiet, unpublicized work of the true innovators. Next, knowledge of the innovation spreads, largely by word of mouth, and perhaps a few obscure articles. Then comes the breakthrough: perhaps a widely read book, or, more likely, cover stories in national magazines and newspapers.

Self-managing teams—the subject of this book, hit the front pages around 1990 with cover stories in both *Fortune* and *Business Week*. These stories provided uncritical praise of the movement toward empowered teams. Many organizations then began to show serious interest in teams.

Now, the predictable next phase of the media cycle is unfolding— stories and books about why teams fail.

In *Business Without Bosses*, we were careful to point out that the use of self-managing teams was not a cakewalk. We have seen the "bumps and warts" that inevitably come with transitions to teams. We wanted to portray a realistic picture of both benefits and costs of teams. Therefore, we set out to write a "second generation" book. The first generation's books can be characterized by "how to do it" checklists, and eternal optimism.

But with *Business Without Bosses*, our intention from the very beginning was to provide a view of teams that reflected the sweaty reality of their implementation. As one executive wrote to us when he read the chapter we wrote about teams in his own organization, "I had forgotten the difficulties we were having at that particular moment in time."

The best way to learn is by sharing the experience of those who have blazed the path. Therefore, we present real-life stories about teams. We provide a series of vicarious site visits that examine teams at a variety of developmental stages, organizational levels, and organizational types.

This book presents the wisdom gained from fifteen years of observation and experimentation. It is not easy to implement self-managed teams. But the nitty-gritty implementation issues can be predicted and overcome. And the results can be extraordinary. Teams will become more and more important in every organization because, despite the so-called "trouble with teams," teams WORK!

Charles C. Manz
Henry P. Sims, Jr.

June 1995

Preface

Business without bosses contradicts the bedrock ideas about how to make organizations work. Your first reaction may be, "Impossible . . . it'll never work." Or, "Terrific . . . I hope my boss is the first to go, the old SOB."

Many of the world's most successful organizations are discovering that the old concept of a single boss can be effectively replaced by the team concept. That's what this book is all about—one of the most important organizational developments to hit business since the industrial revolution: self-managing teams. Teams have the capacity to increase productivity and improve quality significantly, and are an important answer to the competitiveness challenge. Teams do work! Consider the following examples of productivity and quality improvements taken from the chapters that follow:

- A paper mill that used teams to achieve quality and productivity that marked the most successful start-up in the history of the paper industry.

- A mutual fund that reduced crisis telephone response time from 7½ *minutes* to 13 *seconds.*

- A semiconductor manufacturing plant that increased product shipped by 150 percent over a 10-year period, with direct operating employees reduced by 20 percent.

This book is "second generation." It goes beyond surface-level treatments of teams. Many of the most successful applications of teams have not been made public because they were viewed as proprietary information about a competitive advantage. We provide an inside view of self-managing teams at different stages of development in a variety of manufacturing and service organizations. You will learn about a team system credited with substantial productivity and quality gains and about one team implementation that we consider a failure. These remarkable stories about the special challenges of team implementation offer information that can help you make decisions about how teams can fit the needs of your organization. They reveal a powerful new pathway to organizational success by doing business without bosses.

That doesn't mean businesses no longer need managers or leaders. In fact, leadership is a primary ingredient for making teams work. But it's leaders, not bosses, that enable teams to manage themselves to achieve the productivity and quality required today.

Work can be accomplished just as well, actually much better, if we eliminate the old concept of boss. Society has reached a stage where we no longer need people that own almost all the power of a work system and order everyone else around. We don't need people continuously staring over our shoulders, telling us what to do and chewing us out for what we've done wrong. Indeed, the idea of the all-powerful boss is becoming as outdated as the dinosaur.

So how can we make this happen? How can we do business without bosses and actually improve performance? We can do it by organizing people into teams and equipping them with what they need (e.g., training, materials, information, etc.) to do the job themselves. In fact, we will talk about the idea of SuperTeams—teams of workers that manage themselves so well that they deserve the label of "super." A key ingredient to make all this happen is a leader that is the antithesis of the boss. SuperLeaders help others to effectively lead themselves. We will introduce a new view of organizations in which teams develop so that they don't need bosses, but they do need the help of leaders.

We began our research on teams well over a dozen years ago. One of our first efforts to inform the general public about teams was through an interview originally published in *U.S. News and World Report* in 1981. The issues raised in this interview in many ways set the standard for the remarkable team applications seen today, and thus we include a reprint of it in an appendix at the end of this book. After more than a dozen years of studying teams, we are convinced that teams do work! But we hope we give you a realistic preview, including the pain and frustration that typically come with a team implementation. We hope your journey through the team stories in this book will give you a real sense of what teams are all about. The stories include the difficulties and challenges as well as the payoffs.

We like to think of this book as an inside look at empowered work teams without actually leaving your office. Whenever we talk to executives about teams, we always suggest "Go look for yourselves!" The best advocates and most realistic viewpoints about teams come from team members themselves. Also, if you haven't really seen a team in action, many executives have difficulty understanding or believing what's really involved.

Almost every major U.S. corporation is seriously considering work teams.

A decision to implement self-managing teams should not be an automatic copy-cat decision of merely hopping on the fad wagon. This book will explain the tremendous challenges and costs that must be faced when creating empowered work teams, at least in the beginning. But when teams develop as a result of these efforts, the payoffs can be dramatic.

The most important feature of this book is the set of stories about actual organizational experiences with teams. We include accounts from both manufacturing and service industries, we talk about teams at the bottom and teams at the top, and we bring you both successful and unsuccessful teams. Our intention is to provide you with a window through which you can examine the actual experience of teams in several industries and in several forms so that you will be in a position to implement this exciting concept in your own organization if you so choose.

There are many current books on the subject of teams. Most of them cheerlead "rah rah teams," or provide a superficial encyclopedic treatment of the millions of issues surrounding teams. This book was written with a different purpose in mind. It is designed to let you take an inside look into many organizations with *existing* team systems, and let you decide for yourself. We will share with you real life stories of self-managing teams that exist in several different industries. You will experience many of their successes, but, more important, also see their problems and failures. In addition to guarded optimism, we offer a behind-the-scenes view that includes the bumps and warts. We ask that you simply sit back, enjoy your tours of several organizations, and leave the driving to us.

TEAMS AND SUPERLEADERSHIP

In our own previous work, we linked the idea of self-managing teams to overall corporate culture, and especially to organizational leadership. We coined the term *SuperLeadership* to describe the leader who encourages and helps to develop self-leadership in others. We emphasized self-leadership, which we describe as the behavior and patterns of thinking that we use to influence our own effectiveness and performance. A SuperLeader is one who leads others to lead themselves.

A self-managing team is a natural extension of self-leadership. It is a type of collective or group self-leadership. The SuperLeader helps to make it happen by initiating, encouraging, and supporting team self-leadership.

A SuperLeader is one who leads others to lead themselves.

Our first writing on self-management appeared in 1979. Since that time, we have maintained an extremely active interest in research and writing about teams, and have published several dozen articles and papers. All of this work has helped us to understand the amazing potential and formidable challenges of employee self-leadership. SuperLeadership represents a philosophy and practical set of strategies for helping employees with their self-leadership development and practice. We believe it is especially suited for addressing the leadership challenges posed by self-managing teams.

LEARNING FROM STORIES ABOUT TEAMS

In summary, the purpose of our book is to provide you with a straightforward practical inside look at what the team approach is all about. Again, we think of this book as "second generation." A flotilla of teams books has recently come on the market, and most of these are primers or introductions to teams, or, "how to do it" kinds of books. In contrast, we draw on more than a dozen years of experience and provide you with an inside view of real-life teams in action. Specifically, we will tell the story of several organizations that have started teams. You will experience their successes and failures. We will take you on a journey through businesses without bosses. When it is over we hope you will be in a much better position to successfully undertake this same journey within your own organization, should you choose. So let's begin. Happy travels!

CHARLES C. MANZ
HENRY P. SIMS, JR.

August 1993

Acknowledgments

This book is a result of a large extended team. We especially thank our colleagues who helped us with the preparation of the various chapters focusing on specific team stories throughout the book: David Keating, Anne Donnellon, John Newstrom, Barry Bateman, Harold Angle, Frank Shipper, Alan Cheney, and Kenneth Smith. Without their efforts, this book would not exist. Many of these coauthors were the experts or key links critical to the process of developing the inside information for each of the stories.

We are very grateful to the many others who helped make the writing and printing of this book a reality. We thank all the helpful people at Wiley, especially John Mahaney, our editor, who was so instrumental in creating the vision for the book.

Our respective universities—Arizona State University and the University of Maryland–College Park (especially the Business Colleges at each)—have supported our research and writing over the years. Our thanks extend to our deans and chairs: Larry Penley, Rudy Lamone, Luis Gomez-Mejia, and Ed Locke. We especially appreciate the support for manuscript preparation provided by the College of Business Administration at Arizona State University. Jeanette Thomasson provided superb support in preparing the manuscript.

Charles Manz also acknowledges the support of the Harvard Business School, which awarded him a Marvin Bower Fellowship (1988–1989). It was during this time that the research and writing for three chapters in this book was initiated. Hank Sims received support from the Dingman Center at the University of Maryland.

Among the many other colleagues we need to recognize are Chris Argyris, Michael Beyerlein, Tom Cummings, Dennis Gioia, Rollin Glaser, Richard Hackman, Robert House, Ed Lawler, Ted Levitt, Ed Locke, Fred Luthans, Barry Macy, Tom Peters, and Phil Podsakoff. All of these people have significantly affected our thinking and writing over the years. We appreciate Richard Cherry's mentorship and help during the early stages of our research about teams. We continue to be inspired by Tom Peters, who contributed the Foreword to our earlier book.

We owe special thanks to the companies and their managers and employees who allowed us to enter their worlds to learn their unique team stories about business without bosses.

Finally, we thank our families. The energy we have been able to spend writing this and our other books and articles has been greatly facilitated by their support and understanding.

C.C.M.
H.P.S.

Contents

BUSINESS WITHOUT BOSSES

Introduction

Tyrannosaurus Rex: The Boss as Corporate Dinosaur

> In a hierarchical organization, bosses don't do much. . . . They
> just preside and take all the credit. It's criminal. A lot of good
> . . . people are buried down there, and their bosses are happy to
> keep them buried.[1]
> Michael H. Walsh, CEO, Tenneco Corp.

Down with bosses! Up with teams! is the new battle cry of many of
the world's leading organizations in which the traditional role of the
manager is under siege. Bosses limit, control, and too often waste the
potential of employees; teams, in contrast, unleash it. This book is
about how teams conduct business without bosses, a dramatic new
revolution in which the traditional role of managers—bosses—is being
redefined or even eliminated. We show how teams have replaced bosses
in many leading companies and have been successful in producing a new
competitiveness. Today's competitive environment demands intense
improvement in productivity, quality, and response time. Teams can
deliver this improvement. Bosses can't.

For years, bosses have been leading players in business around the
world. They lead through a control system designed to limit employees'
room for error. Bosses occupy central roles and are awarded powerful
status. Bosses have been the kings and, more recently, queens of their
workplace kingdoms. But just as dinosaurs once ruled the earth and
later faded into extinction, the days of bosses may be numbered. They

1

simply don't fit the current business environment of intense international competition, more demanding employees, and complex organizational environments.

Down with bosses! Up with teams! is the new battle cry of the world's leading organizations.

Business Without Bosses examines the unique nature of the way teams have emerged over the past dozen years. Certainly teams can function quite well under the thumb of a strong-minded leader. We think of Mike Ditka, former coach of the Chicago Bears, as an example of a boss who demanded compliance and obedience from his players. By many standards, he was an effective leader, and his team did win a Super Bowl championship. But the way teams have emerged in the business sector is not like the Ditka teams. Teams have leaders but generally not bosses in the traditional sense.

Teams have evolved into a uniquely American style of participative management, but they can be successfully applied around the world. Teams don't need bosses, at least the old type of boss. They develop the capacity for managing and leading themselves. They furnish the initiative, the sense of responsibility, the creativity, and the problem solving from within. When they live up to these ideals, teams are uniquely self-reliant. They don't need a boss.

When we use the word *boss*, we typically mean an individual who influences subordinate employees through such leader behaviors as command, instruction, and top-down goal assignments, frequently accompanied by a healthy dose of reprimand and intimidation—A "do it my way or else!" approach. Bosses can generate compliance, especially in the short term. They have a tendency to create "yes persons" who are willing to comply but lack initiative and creativity. With a boss, the locus of innovation is always top down. Subordinate employees seldom venture forth with their own creative ideas. Their mental powers are centered on trying to say and do as the boss wishes.

In the new wave sweeping across the country, many bosses are being swept away or converted by this powerful force. In their place are teams of employees who serve as their own managers—their own bosses. This new organizational form goes by many labels: self-managing teams, self-directing teams, autonomous and semiautonomous work groups, empowered teams, and many others. We call the really effective ones self-managing SuperTeams because they produce remarkable quality, productivity, innovation, and just plain good business, and they do it without bosses. In our previous book, *SuperLeadership*, we described SuperLeaders, who lead others to lead themselves to high performance. Empowerment, especially team empowerment, is central to creating effective self-leadership. We see effective self-managing teams as an integral part of the philosophy of SuperLeadership. Indeed we view them as SuperTeams.

Teams don't have bosses. They do have leaders . . . SuperLeaders.

Teams don't have bosses, but they do have leaders. No successful team is without leadership. Team leadership positions are sometimes emergent (elected) and sometimes appointed. They frequently have new names, like "coordinator," "facilitator," "coach," and even "team leader." This new form of leadership also demands a new set of behaviors, which we are only beginning to understand from the emerging research. For example, effective team leaders encourage their team to set their own goals and solve their own problems. Being a "boss" is not part of the behavioral repertoire.

A new wave is sweeping across the country—self-managing teams.

If you are currently part of a company where management is resisting the trend and bosses refuse to stop bossing, consider this: Great, powerful, and apparently invulnerable dinosaurs once roamed the earth, seemingly invulnerable to extinction, but they did not evolve and now they no longer live and breathe. We believe the time has come when bosses need to evolve into something else. Our previous book called this "something else" a SuperLeader—one who leads others to lead themselves. SuperLeaders create SuperTeams where everyone on the team is important and makes a significant contribution. In this book, we provide a window to see how several organizations have created

SuperTeams to pursue the tremendous competitive advantages of doing business without bosses. If the bosses of your organization don't make this evolution, your business, and with it your job, may be the next to go the way of the dinosaur.

Where bosses refuse to stop bossing, the organization and jobs may be next to go the way of the dinosaur.

LET'S GET REALISTIC: TEAMS ARE NOT ALWAYS SUPERTEAMS!

Although we are unabashed advocates, we hope we don't see the world of teams through rose-colored glasses. The stories in this book present a realistic view. Certainly we extol the virtues of teams, but we also bring forward the troubles, the problems, the issues, and the challenges that frequently accompany team implementation. In other words, we also describe the bumps and "warts." Our idealism and philosophy are tempered by a good dose of realism.

We write about the good things, but we also describe the bumps and warts.

Thus, not all the teams described in this book are truly SuperTeams, those that control their own decision making, are generally self-managing, and are effective and successful. In fact, some of the teams examined in this book may seem ordinary or are struggling and experiencing frustration. But in the end, our aim and our hope is to provide a learning opportunity that draws on both success and failure so that readers will be further down the road toward creating their own SuperTeams.

WHAT IS A TEAM? WHAT DO TEAMS DO?

Work designs based on self-management tend to give employees a high degree of autonomy and control over their immediate behavior. Teams are one type of the many forms of employee participation that have been developed in the United States. These include organizational approaches such as the following:

- Suggestion boxes
- Employee surveys
- Job enrichment
- Quality circles
- Gainsharing
- Self-managed teams
- Integrated high-involvement cultures

Clearly, there is considerable distance between a rather superficial participative approach like suggestion boxes and a completely integrated high-involvement culture that cuts across all levels of the organization. Self-managing teams fall near the sophisticated end of this continuum and, in fact, are a rather fundamental change from the traditional organization.

Typically, the employees organized into teams complete a whole or a distinct part of a product or service. They make decisions on a wide range of issues, often including such traditional management prerogatives as who will perform which task, solving quality problems, settling conflicts between members on the team, and selecting team leaders. Following are some typical team responsibilities (these responsibilities were especially inspired by the story discussed in Chapter 2):

Self-timekeeping	Recording quality
Analyzing quality problems	Maintaining in-process inventory control
Assigning jobs	Solving technical problems
Training team members	Adjusting production schedules
Redesigning production processes	Resolving internal conflicts
Setting team goals	Preparing annual budgets
Assessing internal performance	

Electing internal team
leader

Testing for competency

Intrateam liaison

Selecting team
members

Team designs vary so much across companies that it's difficult to find one commonly accepted definition of the team approach. It seems to be more of an overall philosophy and approach to work design than a tightly defined set of rules. In fact, part of the essence of the team approach is to encourage each set of employees to find their own way, their own kind of self-managing team that best fits their own situation and team members. Most of all, the team approach is an attempt to utilize more fully the organization's human resources at all levels of the organization.

A typical objective of a work team is to improve productivity for the organization and the quality of working life for employees. Sometimes the dignity and freedom workers receive is especially publicized, but the drive toward productivity and competitiveness is always a constant theme.

Richard Hackman at Harvard University has described teams as having a distinct, recognizable task that workers can identify with (e.g., be able to service all of a mutual fund's customer's needs); members with a variety of skills related to the group task; discretion over issues such as how the work is done, scheduling the work, and assigning tasks; and compensation and performance feedback for the group as a whole.

The early days of the team system were heavily influenced by a concept known as sociotechnical systems (STS) theory, which emphasizes the need to optimize both the social and technical aspects of work. Typically, an STS analysis results in a shift to performing work in groups; technology and people are matched together in clusters, sometimes known as autonomous work groups (teams). The main rationale is that teams can more effectively apply resources to deal with the total variance (changes and unpredictable events) in work conditions than can individuals acting on their own. Today, the formal analysis techniques of STS are found less frequently, but the philosophy of matching the technical system and the social system remains and is an important part of successful team design.

NO, IT'S NOT JAPANESE MANAGEMENT

The team concept we describe has emerged as a distinctly Western phenomenon (teams have been used in the United States, Canada, Europe, and Mexico), although it's frequently confused with so-called Japanese management. Both are often associated with the idea of participatory management, but each approach is targeted at a quite different population, with distinct cultural values. In our attempts to understand the team system, we have traveled to Japan and read extensively about Japanese management systems. Our main conclusion is that the West would be better served by attempting to learn from successful experiences with our own self-managing teams rather than looking to the Japanese for innovative organizational philosophies. The rationale and early successes with team designs originated in the United States and Europe and better fit Western cultures, although they can be successfully applied around the world.

This is not a book about Japanese management. It's about teams, especially U.S. teams.

Most of all, the team concept is beginning to show proven worth for improving productivity, quality, and employee quality of work life, among other payoffs. It is an approach that is designed to take advantage of the strengths of Western culture and history. Teams in the United States, for example, take advantage of the individualism and diversity inherent in the culture.

WHY TEAMS?

We suspect that the notion of teams has reached the stage of the recurring management fads that occasionally sweep the United States. Therefore, some team applications are being undertaken simply because "it's the thing to do," with little thought given to how the approach fits a particular organization, a sure recipe for failure. Nevertheless, there are some solid reasons that teams make good sense:

Increased productivity

Improved quality

Enhanced employee quality of work life

Reduced costs

Reduced turnover and absenteeism

Reduced conflict

Increased innovation

Better organizational adaptability and flexibility

From a management viewpoint, productivity is typically the main reason to implement a team system. Teams are a way to undertake continuous improvement designed to increase productivity. Chapter 2 relates the story of a team-oriented battery plant that can produce its product at a 30 percent savings when compared with battery plants organized in the traditional manner.

Today, teams are often seen as a critical element to a total quality management (TQM) program. The story of the Texas Instruments Malaysia plant that uses teams as the capstone of a TQM program that has resulted in spectacular gains in quality over several years is the subject of Chapter 7.

Sometimes the implementation of teams is motivated by a humanistic ideology. That is, teams are seen as an important way for employees to find satisfaction and dignity in the work—in essence, an enhanced employee quality of work life. Chapter 4 presents evidence of substantially improved work satisfaction that is clearly linked to teams at IDS Financial Corporation.

Teams also typically breed reduced conflict between management and labor. Frequently, the number of grievances is substantially reduced subsequent to a successful team implementation. Chapter 8 describes how an entire organization, AES Corporation, uses teams to enhance its adaptability and flexibility, and Chapter 6 tells the story of how W L. Gore created an entire organizational concept that is directed toward fast-paced innovation.

All of these reasons are important, but as researchers and authors, we believe that issues of productivity and quality—the important elements of competitiveness—are the most important drivers. In the end, the team approach will be adopted only if teams really do work.

Recent years have brought many challenges for Western organizations. Intense international competition, a work force that demands more from work than simply a means for making a living, and the increasing complexity of technical knowledge and information flows have all pressured companies to explore innovative ways of using human resources more effectively. Among the more noteworthy and promising approaches is the concept of self-managing teams.

Traditional approaches to managing human resources have tended to emphasize control from above. Early work system designs tended to treat people as relatively fixed components of a large machine. The bureaucratic form of organization tends to treat people as interchangeable parts rather than unique human resources. Bureaucracy deemphasizes the full use of human resources in favor of a maintenance of stability and status quo. Unfortunately, maintaining the status quo is incompatible with the innovation required for continuous improvement.

When international competition was not strong and when employees were less demanding of power and fulfillment, top-down control was sufficient for organizational success. Now, however, employees are asking that their work provide them personal growth, fulfillment, and dignity from their work, and the emergence of the global marketplace has forced organizations to consider new ways of dealing with the competitive challenge.

Human resources are critical for the development and implementation of organizational strategy. Leadership has been elevated to a more significant status. Corporations are beginning to view people as an investment to be nurtured rather than a cost to be minimized. Teams have emerged as a prominent and pragmatic vehicle to enhance competitiveness through people.

WHAT DO WORKERS WANT?

Each generation is different from previous ones.[2] The generation receiving most attention now is the large group born between the mid-1940s

9

and the 1960s, who grew to maturity during a time of unprecedented prosperity and social turmoil and are variously called the "baby boomers," the "now generation," the "new breed," the "new values worker," and the " '60s kids." As they matured, campus unrest, the controversial Vietnam War, affluence, and societal conditions stimulated a revolution of changing values and mores in the United States. Baby boomers have a set of life and work values that are very different from that of their parents and grandparents. Most of all, they are less tolerant of bosses. They also have lower overall job satisfaction and less desire to lead or manage, move up the organizational hierarchy, and defer to authority. They believe that they are entitled to a "good" job, have a desire to control their own destiny, and have a low absenteeism threshold.[3] Additionally, they have a lower respect for authority and greater desire for self-expression, personal growth, and self-fulfillment. In other words, today's workers are not satisfied to report to work merely for the paycheck. They want something more—and teams can supply it. Teams foster a sense of dignity, self-worth, and a greater commitment to achieving the performance that makes an organization competitive.

Baby boomers have a desire to control their own destiny.

To complicate matters, an even newer set of workers, frequently described as the "baby busters," is now entering the work force. These employees carry yet another set of values and expectations that are significantly different from those of traditional organizations. They are slower to commit and less loyal to organizations. (It's also true that organizations are less loyal to employees.) They were recently described in this way: "They don't bow to any authority. Younger workers will not respect you just because you're the *boss*. They want to know why they're being asked to do things. They question authority, and they have a disregard for hierarchies."[4] They were also described as competitive and as desiring an opportunity to learn and have fun at work.

These characteristics of the new employee generations, when coupled with rises in education and standards of living during this century, pose major challenges for organizations. The new workers' aspirations for self-fulfillment cannot be met by conventional approaches of the past. Teams have a special capacity to answer the needs of the new generation of employees.

Young workers will not respect you just because you're the *boss*.

This is not a new idea. Over ten years ago *Business Week* concluded that "U.S. industry must reorganize work and its incentives to appeal to new worker values, rather than try to retrofit people to work designs and an industrial relations system of 80 years ago."[5] The newer employees have an especially acute need to be treated as valuable and respected contributors and to be given the opportunity to learn, develop, and influence their work and their organizations. We believe self-managing work teams come closer to hitting the nail on the head in meeting these demands than any other tested work system alternative. They break down the traditional, hierarchical, boss-based system and provide employees with the freedom to grow and gain in respect and dignity. With teams, employees control and manage themselves and really make a difference. The message is simple: If you plan on staying in business into the next century, you had better consider teams. Otherwise, you will find yourself swimming upstream against the waves of change fueled by younger workers.

SHIFTING MANAGERIAL PHILOSOPHY

One dilemma frequently encountered in changing to self-managing teams arises because of the transition needed in managerial thinking and philosophy. Empowering lower levels in the organization can be a very unnerving process for managers, who may perceive it as a threat to their own status and power. In addition, leading self-managing employees calls for new management and leadership perspectives and strategies that often do not seem to come naturally to bosses who cut their own teeth in a traditional hierarchical system. Indeed, the transition to employee self-management can be a troubling process for the managers of the self-managing.

THE HISTORICAL EMERGENCE OF TEAMS

Clearly, the notion of teams has had a different impact on the various sectors of our work society. The most extensive experience derives from the manufacturing sector, where this concept was introduced in the 1960s. In the manufacturing sector, it's no longer a question of whether or why to use teams but of fine-tuning to specific sites. The service sector has significantly lagged the manufacturing sector in adoption of teams, but experimentation is well underway. Competitiveness has started to become a hot issue in service, and we expect to see greater intolerance for poor quality service. The IDS case we report in Chapter 4 is an example of the potential of teams in the service sector. While we still have much to learn, teams in the service sector are likely to be the most exciting applications of the 1990s.

The sector that has used the team approach least is the public/government sector. We do see a few sporadic examples (for example, see Tom Peters's program "Excellence in the Public Sector," shown on PBS). The U.S. Office of Personnel Management seems to be offering preliminary encouragement for experimentation with teams in government, but we expect to see only limited progress in the 1990s unless a major shift away from traditional bureaucratic thinking occurs.

In 1990, Edward Lawler, director of the Center for Organizational Effectiveness at the University of Southern California, estimated that about 7 percent of U.S. companies were currently using some form of self-managing teams.[6] Only a decade earlier, he had estimated in personal conversations to us that about 150 to 250 work sites were using teams. Clearly, the number of companies using teams has grown considerably. We believe that nearly every major U.S. company is currently trying or considering some form of empowered work teams somewhere in their organization. Our own informal estimate is that by the end of the decade, 40 to 50 percent of the U.S. work force may work in some kind of empowered teams. Hundreds of applications have taken place across industries in multiple settings including:

pet food plant	coal mines
parts manufacturing	auto manufacturing
paint manufacturing	supply warehouse

| paper mills | insurance offices |
| financial offices | government organizations |

The Procter & Gamble Company is generally considered an important U.S. pioneer in applying teams to their operations. Their work began in the early 1960s, although it was not publicized and virtually escaped media attention. P&G saw the team approach as a significant competitive advantage and through the 1980s attempted to deflect attention away from its efforts. The company thought of its knowledge about the team organization as a type of trade secret and required consultants and employees to sign nondisclosure statements. Nevertheless, Procter & Gamble's successes with teams received considerable off-the-record attention from a small group of consultants across the country who were inspired by the P&G success and learned techniques through an informal network. Many of them originally worked at P&G and were attracted away to other companies by lucrative job offers because of their unique knowledge and expertise.

Through the 1970s and 1980s, General Motors Corporation was also a locus of active experimentation with teams and was significantly less secretive than Procter & Gamble. Many of the GM team implementations have been very successful and have served as models for other changes around the country. These experiments ultimately led to the Saturn experiment, currently GM's most successful division.

GM remains an interesting enigma, however; it is a textbook case of how success with teams at one location does not necessarily transfer to another location within a huge corporation. (Further, teams are not the sole answer to the competitiveness challenge.) Diffusing the team concept throughout large corporations has proven to be a considerable challenge. Also, although specific GM manufacturing plants have been on the cutting edge of employee self-management, many analysts would suggest that the corporate level has maintained a more traditional top-down, control-based management mentality.

General Motors remains an interesting enigma

Other prominent companies have been active with teams, among them Gaines, Cummins Engine, Digital Equipment, Ford, Motorola,

Tektronix, General Electric, Honeywell, LTV, Caterpillar, Boeing, Monsanto, AT&T, and Xerox.

We might also note, with some sadness and regret, that on our own turf (academia) the business and psychology professors are largely playing catch-up in their theoretical development and empirical investigations about teams. Companies such as Procter & Gamble and General Motors have been out there doing it, but, until recently, we have noted the absence of self-managing teams in business organizational behavior curricula. The notion of teams is starting to appear in management textbooks, but it seems to us a half-dozen years late. Clearly, we need more attention to teams in our educational institutions in both the research and teaching arenas.

Finally, at the beginning of the 1990s, the topic of teams had reached the front page. *Fortune* magazine featured a cover story, "Who Needs a Boss?" about teams in the May 7, 1990, issue,[7] and *Business Week* also featured a cover story about teams in their July 10, 1989, issue.[8] Even Dan Rather speaks about "self-directed" teams. In a recent evening news segment he reported that about 7 percent of the major corporations in the United States and Canada are using empowered teams.

Until recently, teams have generally been ignored by the popular media.

Although it's taken some time, teams have clearly reached the stage of becoming a popular "fad" with all the accompanying advantages and disadvantages, but we believe they will pass the test of time and prove to be enduring. We think that teams are here to stay, and that they constitute a fundamental change in the way we go about work. We suspect the label and approach will evolve and perhaps pass—like all so-called fads—but the fundamental ways that teams do business will remain with us for a long time, mainly because teams are effective. Teams may represent a whole new management paradigm. Perhaps they reflect a new business era as influential as the industrial revolution and are destined to revolutionize work for decades to come.

THE BOTTOM LINE: ARE TEAMS EFFECTIVE?

Evidence that evaluates the effectiveness of self-managing teams can be divided into two categories: qualitative evidence, often reported in the popular press, and more rigorous scientific data, derived from well-designed quantitative research.[9]

Business Week claims that teams can increase productivity by 30 percent or more and can also substantially improve quality.[10] Other examples reported in the press include an Alcoa plant in Cleveland, where a production team came up with a method for making forged wheels for vans that increased output 5 percent and cut scrap in half. At Weyerhaeuser, the forest-products company, a team of legal employees significantly reduced the retrieval time for documents. At Federal Express, a thousand clerical workers, divided into teams of five to ten people, helped the company reduce service problems by 13 percent in 1989. At Rubbermaid, a multidisciplinary team from marketing, engineering, and design developed a new product line in 1987; sales in the first year exceeded projections by 50 percent.[11]

Corning eliminated one management level at its corporate computer center, substituting a team adviser for three shift supervisors and producing $150,000 in annual savings and better service. Perceptions of autonomy and responsibility among workers increased because they felt they experienced more meaningful and productive work.[12] In an insurance firm, change to automation led to a shift from functional organizational design to self-managing teams, requiring redesigned contingencies to support organizational goals. A twenty-four-month follow-up found improved work structure, flows, and outcomes.[13]

Also, throughout this book we describe several organizations that have enjoyed impressive payoffs with teams in both the long and short term. In Chapter 2, for example, we tell the story of a mature General Motors automobile battery plant organized around teams in which company officials reported productivity savings of 30 to 40 percent when compared with traditionally organized plants. In Chapter 3 we tell how teams helped Lake Superior Paper Company enjoy possibly the most successful start-up in the history of the paper industry. In Chapter 1 we describe the very beginning adjustments of management to the team approach that a few short months later was credited with productivity improvements of 10 percent per year, cost savings of 10 to 20 percent of earnings, and customer service quality levels of over 99 percent.

Considerable data indicate the effectiveness of teams. Nevertheless, not all the evidence, especially from more rigorous academic research, is completely supportive. Perhaps the difficulty of evaluating the team concept in terms of any hard scientific data was best expressed by John Miner:

> The results are often positive. It is hard to predict whether the outcomes will be greater output, better quality, less absenteeism, reduced turnover, fewer accidents, greater job satisfaction, or what, but the introduction of autonomous work groups is often associated with improvements. It is difficult to understand why a particular outcome such as increased productivity occurs in one study and not in another, and why, on some occasions, nothing improves. Furthermore, what actually causes the changes when they do occur is not known. The approach calls for making so many changes at once that it is almost impossible to judge the value of the individual variables. Increased pay, self-selection of work situations, multiskilling, with its resultant job enrichment and decreased contact with authority almost invariably occurs in autonomous work groups.[14]

In another report, researchers attempted a rigorously scientific review of the effectiveness of the team approach. Despite 1,100 studies conducted in actual organizations, they concluded that "there are not many well-designed studies that evaluate the impact of self-managed groups."[15]

Perhaps the most revealing scientific study of the bottom-line effect of teams is contained in a recent paper from Barry Macy and associates at the Texas Center for Productivity and Quality of Work Life.[16] Their analysis contrasted the success of various changes involving human resources, work structure, and technology—for example, training, reward systems, and work teams. Very strong effects, especially in terms of financial outcomes, were observed with team applications. The Macy study is one of the first rigorous scientific efforts that shows the clear financial effect of the team approach in dozens of organizations.

The most revealing scientific study shows the clear financial effect of the team approach.

A vast body of experience lies unreported in the scientific literature. Those close to the self-management movement informally report substantial productivity gains and cost savings that typically range from 30 to 70 percent when compared with traditional systems. Self-managing teams have the potential to exert substantial effects on the bottom line. Perhaps the notion was captured best by Charles Eberle, a former vice-president at Procter & Gamble, who speaks with the advantage of years of practical experience:

> At P&G there are well over two decades of comparisons of results—*side by side*—between enlightened work systems and those I call traditional. It is absolutely clear that the new work systems work better—*a lot better*—for example, with 30 to 50 percent lower manufacturing costs. Not only are the tangible, measurable, bottom line indicators such as cost, quality, customer service and reliability better, but also the harder-to-measure attributes such as quickness, decisiveness, toughness, and just plain resourcefulness of these organizations.[17]

RESISTANCE TO TEAMS

A cover story in *Business Week* asked: "The gains in quality are substantial—so why isn't it spreading faster?" Why do companies and employees resist the change to more self-managing teams? There are several philosophical and practical barriers to the ready acceptance of the team concept. Many of these stem from discomfort with the unknown and general resistance to change. Some of the more notable resistances that frequently arise with a change to teams follow.[18]

Emphasis on Individuality

In the United States, we have a strong political and personal tradition of individual freedom that at times runs counter to the collective nature of teamwork. For both managerial and nonmanagerial employees, an emphasis on team values threatens not only their traditional views of work but their approach to life. Many employees also have difficulty adjusting to the idea of working without a traditional boss or supervisor after so many years of dependence. We recently learned of a case where a large burly production worker, after learning about his company's move to self-managing teams, banged his fist on a table and demanded his right to have a boss to tell him what to do.

Distrust

With a history of management-induced fads and poor management of industrial relations, some companies have no immediate credibility with first-line employees, especially unionized employees, to earn the trust needed to implement team processes. If management sees team development as an expense rather than an investment and employees see teams as another attempt to co-opt employees to management's views, an attempted shift to team values and work will likely fail. It is not surprising that many stories of successful team efforts have come from threatened companies or industries, where workers and management were forced to confront and discard traditional distrust in favor of teams.

Lost Employment Opportunities for Middle Management

For managers, a shift to teams and to the corresponding flatter organizations reduces their opportunities for advancement in the traditional organizational hierarchy, if only because there is no longer much of a hierarchy. But certainly there are economic factors, not just a movement to teams, that have threatened the career prospects and aspirations of many managers. Downsizing and delayering will continue whether teams are used or not.

Lack of Empathy and Understanding

The management of self-managing teams requires the ability to listen, to change views, to empathize, and to change basic behavior patterns.

18

Without an adequate investment in the training and development of social work skills, team development will be retarded or even thwarted.

Managerial Resistance

Managers who have been trained to manage in a forceful or threatening way may not readily accept the concept of teams. The change to a team approach results in a variety of disincentives to the traditional, hard-charger manager.

A PREVIEW OF BUSINESS WITHOUT BOSSES

Our purpose in writing this book is to give you an insider's tour of several actual team experiences. Think of these stories as armchair site visits. Here's a preview of the stories we will tell.

Chapter 1, "On the Road to Teams: Overcoming the Middle Management Brick Wall," is about probably the biggest challenge to successful implementation of teams. Managers (especially first-line supervisors) are frequently the most threatened and resistant to the whole team concept. Their power and status as boss becomes vulnerable, and they may have difficulty learning a new organizational role that is of central importance to team development. These managers in the middle risk the possibility that doing their job well may mean working themselves out of a job. Chapter 1 presents the struggles and transition of middle managers in a warehouse operation of Charrette Corporation as they prepare to lead workers into a team structure.

Chapter 2, "The Day-to-Day Team Experience: Roles, Behaviors, and Performance of Mature Self-Managed Teams," looks at a relatively mature team system at a General Motors plant that produces maintenance-free automobile batteries. The focus of the chapter is on the day-to-day behaviors, activities, and conversations of employees working in teams. It describes what teams look like and are capable of once they have developed their necessary work and team skills and the system has become relatively stable. In addition, it reports on the leadership characteristics of team leaders and coordinators that enable the creation of business without bosses.

Chapter 3, "The Good and the Bad of Teams: A Practical Look at Successes and Challenges" provides a practical and balanced look at teams in a paper mill owned and operated by Lake Superior Paper Company. The teams examined in this chapter are still at the relatively early stage of their development. The story includes many significant successes, as well as many challenges that need to be resolved. This chapter is particularly useful for gaining a sense of the realities of the struggle to get a team system up and running.

Chapter 4, "The Early Implementation Phase: Getting Teams Started in the Office," examines the launch of a team system at IDS Financial Services. The story of the planning, prelaunch, and initial introduction of teams is related in detail, including the implementation decision, the involvement of the external consultant, and the formation of the primary committees and groups that have guided the transition. This chapter provides an understanding of what needs to be done to create business without bosses from the beginning and a sense of the relevance of teams for service organizations. It also contains a recent description of the organization and the benefits it has reaped from a team approach.

Chapter 5, "The Illusion of Self-Management: Using Teams to Disempower," looks at an application of self-managing teams as a mechanism to increase control of employees in an independent insurance firm. The story raises the caution that just because we use the word "self-management," it does not automatically follow that employees are empowered and that business without bosses is achieved. The champion of the introduction of self-managing teams in this company, the CEO, publicly espoused a strong commitment to the philosophy of employee empowerment, but, in reality, the system created only an illusion of self-management. After careful study, it became clear that the team system was actually used to *reduce* employee discretion and personal control.

Chapter 6, "Self-Management Without Formal Teams: The Organization as Team," describes an alternative way of establishing business without bosses and employee self-management without formally established teams. The approach of the very successful W. L. Gore corporation is examined in detail, revealing a fascinating system of self-developing teams that emerge only as needed. A system without bosses or managers but with lots of leaders is at the heart of this success story.

The company has no "employees," only "associates" who team up directly with whomever they need to get the job done, without worrying about going through a chain of command. An inside view is provided of one of the most advanced self-leadership systems we have seen so far, where lots of teamwork takes place but teams are not formally defined by management. In fact, the term "unmanagement" (which implies the existence of "unbosses") is used to describe the Gore approach to business without bosses.

Chapter 7, "Teams and Total Quality Management: An International Application," looks at teams as part of an overall total quality management (TQM) effort. In this successful application at a Texas Instruments plant in Malaysia, teams are viewed as only one piece, albeit an important one, of an overall effort dedicated to total quality management. Also, the plant employs a rich and culturally diverse work force. This story reveals a striking openness to combining good ideas originating from many sources to create an optimal team-based work system. Total quality management, cultural diversity, and striving to create an organizational hybrid from the best manufacturing ideas in the world are the main themes of this fascinating story.

Chapter 8, "The Strategy Team: Teams at the Top," emphasizes the importance of teamwork in developing corporate strategy. Many interlocking teams are used at AES Corporation to accomplish the "strategy-making" process. This chapter especially focuses on the importance of upper-level (executive) teams. Although teams and teamwork are a central part of the organization's culture and philosophy at all levels, a multilayered executive "onion" of overlapping committees provides the core of this impressive company, where strategy is driven by core values. This chapter represents an important reminder that teams are not just for lower-level employees but are appropriate at the top as well.

Chapter 9, "Business Without Bosses Through Teams: What Have We Learned? Where Are We Going?" identifies the primary lessons and challenges suggested by the team stories in this book. The book includes a diverse set of self-managing team systems across both manufacturing and service companies, representing a wide range of management philosophies. Yet there are some common prescriptions and cautions that flow from this fascinating set of stories. This final chapter outlines lessons and prescriptions that can serve as an important starting point for organizations considering or already grappling with the team approach. In particular, a beginning road map is provided for establishing very successful businesses without bosses. Overall, the stories reveal how in some very successful organizations the Boss has become an obsolete Corporate Tyrannosaurus Rex ready for a dinosaur graveyard. Now, prepare to begin your site visits to observe *Businesses Without Bosses*. We hope you find your journey interesting as well as informative.

Chapter 1

On the Road to Teams: Overcoming the Middle Management Brick Wall

This chapter addresses the biggest obstacle to success with teams: the middle management brick wall. Success or failure is often determined before the teams are put into place. Many companies decide to go into teams but don't know what to do next. This chapter deals with the next step. It tells how the managers of a warehouse operation prepared themselves for conducting business without bosses—how they moved themselves beyond bossing to facilitating and leading. The story captures the essence of the challenge for traditional managers and supervisors (bosses) who learn that their job is about to be changed forever.

This chapter was written by Charles C. Manz, David Keating, and Anne Donnellon.

The decision to adopt teams and to move toward doing business without bosses requires managers within the organization to make significant adjustments. Passing of power and control to lower levels in the organization can be an intimidating process for managers, stemming largely from their own sense of loss of status and power. In addition, leading self-managing employees calls for new perspectives and strategies, which may not come naturally for those involved. Indeed, the transition toward employee self-management can be an uncertain and troubling process for the managers of the self-managing.[1]

Leading self-managed employees calls for new perspectives that do not seem to come naturally.

This critical factor strongly influences the self-managing process yet is often overlooked in the research and writing on self-managing teams. In this chapter we address this issue in some detail and examine the transition difficulties of managers who are making such an organizational change, especially their struggles with the concept of having their workers manage themselves.[2]

THE TRANSITION TO SELF-MANAGING TEAMS

Charrette Corporation, located in the greater Boston area, is a nonunion wholesale distributor and retailer of architectural, engineering, and commercial art supplies and furnishings, with a current annual sales volume exceeding $50 million. It was cofounded in 1964 by the company's current chairman and president, who together totally own the company.

Our focus was on the organization's warehouse distribution center operation. The distribution center is broken into four basic parts: receiving/stocking, order filling, order packing, and shipping. The study centered on managers directly involved with the order-filling and order-packing work force, approximately 65 persons.

The core management team consisted of seven persons: the director of operations, who is responsible for coordinating all aspects of the distribution center's four basic parts; the day and night managers who oversee all day-to-day operational details of order filling and order packing; and four day and night order-packing and -filling supervisors, who report directly to those two managers. The four supervisors handle all minute-to-minute concerns regarding work force and production flow and because of heavy order volume, they often fill and pack orders.

Most of the core management team had been with the company for at least four years, about five times longer than the average worker, and most had come up through the ranks of order filling and order packing. The usual management style had been a traditional autocratic approach with a punitive emphasis. The typical perception of a good manager/leader in the organization in the past was one of doing "whatever it took" to get the job done, with a heavy emphasis on exerting tight control over the work force.

The old management approach was not paying off. The operations efficiency and productivity levels were problematic. Current operating statistics on an annualized basis estimated absenteeism to be about 10 percent, turnover 250 percent, productivity utilization 60 percent, and errors at about 1.8 percent of all orders. Average cost of inefficiencies was estimated to be about 30 percent of earnings. Despite the clear need for change, the move to a self-managing team approach, decided upon by the CEO and a consultant, posed a direct conflict in management philosophy with the old management system and required significant unlearning on the part of the managers.

Several work force characteristics made this an especially interesting organization to study in terms of the transition of management thinking. First, the average age of the employees involved in the change was nineteen, significantly younger than many other self-managed team applications. A majority of the workers were recent high school graduates or dropouts. Coupled with the relatively young age of the work force were several other sources of tension and personal difficulties for the workers. There was some covert tension within the racially mixed work force that consisted of approximately 73 percent white, 12.5 percent black, and 14.5 percent Hispanic. This tension showed up in hostile written exchanges on the bathroom walls and some uncooperative behavior during normal work operations. Often white male employees mocked the speech and behavior patterns of their minority counterparts. Rarely did white and blacks work together or socialize. In addition, several employees had been arrested for possession and dealing drugs.

The new self-management system required significant unlearning on the part of the managers.

All of these factors made an organizational change to the concept of worker self-managing teams particularly challenging for members of management. It was apparent to management that organizational change was needed to improve employee productivity and morale, but whether this young and troubled work force could handle a self-managed environment was uncertain. The managers' role in the transition and functioning of these teams would be critical to achieving a successful implementation.

GATHERING INFORMATION

We used several methods for gathering information in studying the managers' transition. First, the second author of this chapter (Keating) was a consultant to the company. He proposed and paved the way for implementing the transition to self-managed teams. (Enlisting the help of an outside consultant is not a necessity for introducing teams, but many organizations find the support and guidance of a consultant to be useful.) He worked with the company for a little more than two months. During this period, he analyzed the existing operating approach, proposed a self-managed work team design, and then worked directly with the core management team to facilitate their preparation for the change. This close work enabled very rich, first-hand observation and interaction with the management team during its transition toward a self-management philosophy. Detailed documentation was kept in a journal during this process.

In addition, multiple interviews and discussions were conducted with individual members of the management team from the time the proposed change approach was accepted until implementation was begun. Some of the key interactions of managers concerning managing in an employee self-managing environment were videotaped. The taping focused primarily on manager role plays as they began to practice and converse about managing workers who are being encouraged and helped to be increasingly self-managing. This provided an especially detailed source of insight into the managers' thoughts, feelings and behavior during the transition to self-management.[3]

PRIMARY THEMES OF THE
MANAGERIAL TRANSITION

Our study of the management team's struggle with the pending organizational change identified several primary themes, which we will illustrate by providing examples of the interactions that occurred between members of management during the transition. These episodes not only revealed the process but seemed to provide the raw material for the construction and evolution of the change in management philosophy and action.

Theme 1: Initial Suspicion, Uncertainty, and Resistance

During the transition, the managers felt threatened by and resented the forthcoming change. They were concerned over having what might be viewed as past personal performance failings come to the attention of upper management, they resented the tendency for the change plan to be credited to the consultant, and they were sure that the new system would fail. In other words, they believed that an analysis of the system that revealed a need for change threatened to make them look bad, and they perceived that the new work design plan, even if it worked, would serve only to enhance the image of the consultant and not the managers.

We identified a feeling of threat and resentment toward the forthcoming change.

The day manager led the initial resistance. The existing system, he said, had "evolved over time," and was "designed for maximum flexibility" (that is, *his* flexibility in assigning orders to and maintaining control over the workers). He believed that if a team approach were instituted, orders would not be filled and shipped, since more of the decisions and responsibilities would be left to the employees and out of his control. He feared that missed shipments would cost him his job. In addition, gaining approval from senior management for the new system would require exposing the distribution center's inefficiencies, and he feared that this would cost him his job (especially precious because of a wife, a child, and a baby "on the way"). To overcome this resistance, the consultant had to ensure that this manager was insulated from senior management.

Senior management approved the new approach without firing the day manager, but he continued to resist the change. His response to the news that senior management had approved the change was to throw his cigarette lighter across his desk in disgust. Through the first several days of meetings, he displayed closed body language and offered little to group discussion.

At the end of one of the first days, he directly confronted the consultant with the argument that the design would mainly benefit him—the consultant. After the consultant pointed to the potential benefits to the organization, the manager again raised his accusation of personal gain for the consultant, which the consultant then acknowledged. (This manager later realized the potential positive possibilities of the new system and publicly apologized to the consultant. He began making excellent contributions to the change and was often instrumental in helping the core group develop a language for their new roles as facilitators. He was thus given the nickname "Wordman.")

A variety of comments made during these early stages of the transition indicated an attachment to the company's traditional style of management. One manager emphasized the inadequacies of the workers and pointed out, "We have to step in and solve the problem for them." Another manager revealed his impatience with the shortcomings of the work force: "We can't be bothered by people that don't work." In general, the core group's behaviors suggested a belief that their workers were too immature and irresponsible to handle the change.

The managers believed that the workers were too immature and irresponsible to handle the change.

In summary, the initial responses to the change were suspicion, uncertainty, and resistance. Conversations during the early core management meetings placed a significant emphasis on these concerns. These conversations appeared to serve as a venting process for the internal pressure felt by some of the core management group members, and they seemed to be symptomatic of a last-ditch effort to stop the change.

Theme 2: Gradual Realization of the Positive Possibilities in the New System

The second theme was the managers' growing belief that the new system could work. This realization gradually emerged after hours of struggle and discussion about the possibilities and challenges of the team approach. The belief that the workers were competent and responsible emerged as the managers began to grasp the potential advantages of the new system. In addition, the core managers began to recognize that they had to assume a new role as facilitators, moving away from traditional thinking about management.

As they went through their transition, the core managers questioned and tested the boundaries of the new system. Questions ranged from "Can groups really facilitate themselves?" to such basic operational questions as, "Can groups train new people [a task previously assigned only to managers]?" These managers gradually switched from questioning their employees' competence to exploring ways of empowering them with the authority to perform management tasks.

In addition, the core group discussed a plan to have workers call customers for feedback on orders for which their group was responsible. The managers, recognizing that the company's success depends on courteous employees and accurate orders, voiced their concern that workers might be vulgar or unable to respond diplomatically to an angry customer. Nevertheless, they decided that it was an idea worth pursuing; this communication with customers would help build worker identification with and empathy for customers—a radical shift away from managers' previous belief that they should "keep the animals in the warehouse as far away from customers as possible!"

The managers decided that having workers call a customer was an idea worth pursuing.

The core managers developed an understanding that the program's success depended on workers' placing significant value on group membership, that is, peer acceptance. This belief grew out of the managers' frustration over their inability to control absenteeism and unprofessional behavior. As they probed the issue with the help of the consultant, they realized that line authority over a worker does not necessarily equate to behavioral control. From this, the managers reached the conclusion that peer pressure often is more effective than managerial threats and that a worker would be less likely to call in sick if he or she had to face team members the next morning.

The core group came to realize that the new system might also change some enjoyable aspects of their old roles, such as identifying and developing rising stars. At first, they were concerned that their new role of facilitator was too indirect to be effective. Over time, they came to accept that as workers became self-managing, they would have more time to develop key people, although in a new manner.

They realized that line authority does not necessarily equate to behavioral control.

Finally, the core group developed an understanding of their new roles as resources to their groups, as well as a support group among themselves. Previously when workers were unsure of what to do, the managers would either tell them what to do or step in and solve the problem themselves. As the core group developed, they created and practiced techniques for facilitating worker problem solving. These techniques centered on asking questions rather than giving answers and allowing workers to make mistakes without reprimand as they struggled to solve problems on their own.

Throughout the whole process, the core group became a resource to itself. In the beginning, they doubted the value of spending so much of their time in discussion. "Well I'm off to group therapy," one manager would quip as he left for the meetings. By the end of the process, they were pleased with their ability to wrestle with complicated issues. They had solved problems that had stumped the department for years and attributed this success to the group process.

The group developed its own informal leaders and inside jokes. One member could always be counted on to supply candy during the three-to four-hour meetings. Other members used humor to break frequent tension. One member became known as "The Tower of Compassion," because of such statements as, "We can't be bothered by people who don't fit in [to the new program]." The group also occasionally engaged in story-telling about important accomplishments of the past.

Officially they named themselves the Advisory Board. Their charter was to create policy and serve as informal judicial review for worker grievances. As a group, they took on increasingly more difficult tasks, including a multimedia presentation (proposing their plan for the new self-managed system) to the company's chairman and senior management.

In summary, conversations and interactions within the management team revealed their gradual realization of the potential benefits of the new system. During this shift in their beliefs and attitudes, the managers learned from and supported each other in a manner most members of the group felt to be more effective than any previous management training.

The facilitation technique centered on asking questions rather than giving answers.

The final two themes reveal our findings from detailed analysis of some of these conversations, particularly the conversations captured on videotape. Our intent is to show how the managers' interaction produced the new roles and behavior required for managing the self-managed.

Theme 3: Wrestling with a New Role

Throughout the process, the core management group wrestled with the question about their new role: What exactly is a facilitator? How is it different from or better than being a manager? They were asking, in other words, How does the philosophy of self-management influence managerial behavior? This influence was seen in frequent references to the self-management philosophy as a guide to communication behavior. These references were mentioned by the managers of the core group, the consultant, and occasionally by the participating managers during role-playing. Whether the managers would grasp the full meaning of this philosophy and alter their image of their role ultimately would determine how effective they would be in managing the self-managed.

In role-playing about a team seeking to remove one of its members, one manager proposed to meet with each of the team members individually to determine the reasons for the request and the degree to which each person supported it. Recognizing this behavior as a violation of the team philosophy, one of his colleagues asked him to consider "what that will do to the group mentality."

Another manager, while practicing his new role as a facilitator, was reminded that "the facilitator's role is not to work with the individual but with the group." The challenge of managing both the individual and the team was not overlooked by these managers, as was obvious when one manager posed the dilemma: "What do we do if a person [whose teammates want him out] wants to stay in the group?" After much discussion of alternative responses, he stated the philosophy that was to guide all such communication with the teams: "So what we all agreed is, no matter what we do, we're gonna do everything on our part to keep the group intact." When another manager proposed dealing with team complaints about a poor performer by saying, "Maybe we say, 'Hey somebody's gotta babysit him; we'll do that on a rotating basis,' " he was quickly reminded that the facilitator role did not include babysitting.

The facilitator's role is not to work with the individual but with the group.

The managers openly explored the motivation for adopting the philosophy of being a facilitator. One manager proposed that "the facilitator has a vested interest in making the group work." Other managers supported this argument by pointing out that the manager's motivation was more than monetary: "This group is his. If they fail, he fails. There's the psychological thing of, 'I failed; I wasn't able to pull this group together.' "

Perhaps the most compelling evidence that the managers recognized and were consciously grappling with their new role was in the following statement: "They know you're in an uncomfortable role, and they're gonna push and push and push, and when you slip, they're gonna say,

'There he goes, acting like a son of a bitch again,' and that's gonna undermine the whole effort. They're gonna look at the whole thing as a manipulative effort.'' This manager clearly understands the challenge of the new role, and he implies that effective performance of the role will depend on the managers' genuine acceptance of the self-management philosophy.

This group is his. If they fail, he fails.

Acting in their new roles as facilitators of self-managing teams, managers must be aware of what the new philosophy logically entails. Two such subthemes were discussed in the conversations we observed. One was the argument that the self-managing teams "can solve anything." The other subtheme dealt with appropriate styles of communicating within the team.

In scenarios that dealt with self-managing teams as potential sources of interpersonal conflict and coordination problems, these managers occasionally had to remind one another of an important aspect of the self-management philosophy: the teams were formed to be problem-solving groups. They proposed language that would remind the teams of this aspect of the new structure. During a role-play, the "facilitator" affirmed his group by saying, "We can solve it." When a member of the group apologized, the facilitator reminded him, "Apologies don't solve problems." Thus, they coached one another in the underlying philosophy of their new role and at the same time identified behavior that would be effective in such a situation.

The subtheme dealing with appropriate styles of communication in the teams appeared to be more of a problem for this group, particularly when serving as a guide to selecting and acting out effective behavior. On a number of occasions, the consultant responded to a role-play by asking the managers to critique and correct the language used by a team member. A manager's response to one role-playing situation was the following:

He just said he "snorted his paycheck," but that's not relevant. It doesn't matter why he's out; his absenteeism is the problem.

You can't let anyone attack him. You've got to let just enough negative energy out to make him realize he's done something wrong that he needs to correct. And anything else is unnecessary and destructive. Insults are unacceptable.

The consultant argued that constructive communication is the goal of facilitation; the facilitator should counter destructive behavior and instruct team members in how to express themselves constructively. One manager, however, expressed concern about the potential for altering the language without solving the problem.

"I don't think that [saying he snorted his paycheck] was an insult . . . and I know he's got a drug problem. I've seen him, and it affects his work."

This interaction and others indicated the tension felt between working to foster open, honest communication of thoughts and feelings and working to block communication that could degenerate into emotional outbursts. The consultant put the problem on the table as a policy issue: "Is it going to be the role of the facilitator to say we're not going to use language that's inflammatory in this room, or do you feel it's the way they express themselves and you shouldn't inhibit that?"

The question of how to act when team members communicated negative emotion honestly was not directly posed or resolved by the consultant or the managers; however, guides to action were articulated, with the managers left to find their own motivation and produce their own responses: "That might be something to apply down the road," "It would be unwise to inhibit them initially, they need to be able to swear to get loosened up."

Theme 4: Learning a New Language

The purpose of the training role-plays during the managers' transition to self-managing teams was to provide opportunities for the managers to rehearse appropriate behaviors for their new roles. The consultant told them, "We want you to have as many possible scenarios as could come up. We want you to be as equipped as possible so you don't sit there and say, 'Good grief! I'm in this new role and I have anarchy on my hands,' and your first reaction is to pull out the fists and go back to being a supervisor again. When that happens, we've lost."

Preparing as a group, they experimented with the new ways of speaking and tested the effectiveness of this new speech with one another. For example, after one role-play, a manager offered the following critique to his colleague: "But doesn't that put me on the defensive again?" Another responded, "That sounds kinda hokey to me."

Your first reaction is to go back to being a supervisor again. When that happens, we've lost.

In these discussions of possible conversations with their teams, the managers and consultant produced action plans, or "scripts," for dealing with various contingencies. These discussions dealt with physical arrangements, word choices and sequences of dialogue, and even audience expectations and reactions.

Prompted by the consultant, one manager began his plan of action for addressing team concerns about a member whose absenteeism was affecting their bonuses by specifying that he would not have the accused person sit next to him, "just to make this individual not feel separated. If he's next to me, they'll be looking at me, and he'll feel their stares."

In the role-play of this interaction, another participant responded to the question of whether a person was entitled to a leave of absence by saying he would need to appeal to "the judicial board [a group created to deal with special issues such as this]." This discussion caused one of the managers to react negatively to the group's name: " 'Judicial board' is kinda strong. Doesn't that sound kinda scary?" Several other possible names for the body were proposed, including the "People's Board." (The interaction concluded with joking references to a popular television show, "The People's Court.") The managers realized that they needed to develop a name that commanded respect yet was not intimidating.

In working to identify appropriate ways for the facilitators to communicate with their groups, the managers recognized that the team context heightened the importance of the words chosen to deal with workers. After one role-play, for example, one manager pointed out,

"But three people [on the team] have a specific agenda they want addressed, and to just skirt around it and not get to the meat of it might be unwise." With this comment, he called his colleagues' attention to the fact that, in team conversations, the facilitator's words must be chosen with regard not just to the self-management philosophy or to creating the desired effect on the focal individual but to the audience of other team members as well. Another manager offered an interesting perspective on the team audience: "They've always seen authority figures, and they've never been invited to be a peer of that person. We're inviting them to be peers with us, and they're not gonna buy that right away." Obviously, he was concerned with the audience's expectations, which are based on prior experience and understanding of the roles each party typically plays. His words served as a sober reminder to his colleagues of the magnitude of change that self-management represented in this company and the challenge of communicating effectively as a facilitator.

By this point in the process, all of the managers were convinced of the challenge they faced as facilitators, and they applied considerable energy to developing and practicing the verbal skills required for effective performance of the facilitator role. They had to establish the underlying motivation for their new role in their own minds, produce new plans to act out when confronted with difficult situations that they anticipated, and stop occasionally to reconsider audience expectations. Another obvious skill was to recall (or improvise) and deliver the right words at the right time.

They applied considerable energy to developing and practicing the verbal skills required for effective performance of the facilitator role.

The role-plays offered an opportunity to practice these skills. Dialogue lines that flowed from their newly developed language like the following were quite common in the conversations: "I'm not here to solve the problem. I'm here to assist *you* in solving the problem." In the group training context, the role-plays also provided opportunities for feedback. For example, when, in the heat of dialogue, one manager used the line, "That's not up to me; it's up to you," he was reminded that the facilitator is also "part of the team, so you should have said, 'It's up to us.' " In self-evaluations, two of the managers said that they shouldn't have used the term "individual."

Although the bulk of their conversations were generally devoted to creating and practicing this new language, the managers and consultant also recognized the need for skill in improvising. As one manager pointed out, "They [the team] will push you. They know you're in an uncomfortable role, and they'll push you to react. It's gonna get heated, confrontational." Other managers proposed ways of developing the improvisational skill to deal with these pressures—for example, "Before you call a meeting, before you go to a meeting, it's up to the facilitator to assess the situation. You should know what's going on with your group; you should be able to assess what topics are gonna come up in the conversation and should come with all the ammunition." The consultant seconded this idea and advised, "Don't get thrown off-guard, and if you are, don't get flustered. Throw it back to the group."

SUMMARY AND CONCLUSIONS

One of the challenging and often-overlooked aspects of implementing a change to self-managing work teams concerns the transition from supervisor to facilitator. Frequently in the literature, the implementation of this innovative work design approach is viewed primarily in terms of the challenges and difficulties posed for workers. When supervisors and managers are considered, it is usually an afterthought—after the implementation has already occurred and when these individuals are trying to go about their business of managing. The initial transition of managers—after they learn about a self-managing system but before it is actually implemented—is critical to the ultimate success of the team approach.

This transition for managers is challenging for two primary reasons: they experience a perceived loss of power and control as they realize that their subordinates are to become their own managers, and they recognize that their repertoire of management skills, often developed over years of experience and struggle, will become somewhat obsolete. Consequently, they are expected to learn a whole new set of managerial skills that they are not certain that they can successfully master and apply. Managers' adjustment to these perceived threats and challenges was the primary focus of our study.

The warehouse distribution center of Charrette Corporation was a good one for examining the adjustments required of managers facing the transition to worker self-management. The employees were part of a very young and perhaps troubled work force. In addition, the dominant traditional management style used in the operation was autocratic, with an emphasis on punishment. Indeed, the managers we studied faced a significant challenge in establishing ways that they could act out a new role to help the system succeed in their organization.

Our findings uncovered several themes in the management team's transition that offer important lessons for other organizations considering such change efforts. They are summarized in the Key Lessons for Creating Business Without Bosses at the end of the chapter.

The story examined here underlines the critical role that supervisory and managerial training fulfills during this sensitive transition. Managers can make or break a team implementation. Training is a critical element that helps to overcome initial suspicion and develop necessary facilitator skills and behaviors. In many ways, this transition might be described as the foundation for the future success or failure of the new work system.

EPILOGUE

The team system at the Charrette Corporation has been in operation for four years. The teams continue to achieve steady productivity improvements (approximately 10 percent per year), and the overall cost savings are approaching 10 to 20 percent of earnings. Quality levels average 99.8 percent of all customer items requested.

The management group, including supervisors, is still in place in the warehouse. The teams themselves have been reduced from five to six members per team to two members per team, but they retain their cross-functional nature; that is, one member picks items from the shelf, and the other packages them. This cross-functionality contributes to the high quality levels being achieved. The management group decided to reduce the team size because of what they described as a need to reduce the communication needs inherent in larger teams. One manager noted, "communication needs get in the way of getting the work done." This viewpoint and decision to reduce team size may indicate some lapse into the prior more traditional management style. Indeed, the transition to doing business without bosses through teams can be a very lengthy and stubborn process.

Nevertheless, the management group indicated that it could have neither achieved nor maintained the productivity, quality assurance, attendance, and turnover goals it has achieved without the system. Today the team system remains operational, effective, and supported by the implementation team, as well as senior management.

Key Lessons for Creating Business Without Bosses

1. The transition to self-managing teams is at least as challenging for middle level managers as for team members.
2. Managers are likely to experience four stages:

   Stage 1: Initial suspicion, uncertainty, and resistance. The move to self-managing teams is frequently viewed as an indication of ineffectiveness in the managers' previous behavior. Also, teams are seen as benefiting someone else (e.g., the consultant) and ultimately destined to fail.

   Stage 2: Gradual realization of the positive possibilities offered by self-managing teams. After hours of struggle and discussion, managers begin to see that teams offer many benefits that go beyond traditional management approaches: constructive peer pressure within teams, employee development of empathy for the customer, freeing up managers' time for developing key people, and others.

   Stage 3: Understanding of their new leadership role. Managers struggle with questions, such as, What is a facilitator? How does self-management influence managerial behavior?

   Stage 4: Learning a new language. The managers develop and rehearse a new vocabulary and new communication scripts for leading self-managed employees. Through role playing, the managers identify and develop the verbal skills that form the core of their new leadership role.

3. Time and effort to help managers are critical for creating successful self-managing teams.
4. Training and learning opportunities to help middle managers through the transition to their new leadership role may be the most powerful ingredient for success with self-managing teams.

The Day-to-Day Team Experience: Roles, Behaviors, and Performance of Mature Self-Managing Teams

This chapter describes the roles, responsibilities, and performance of mature self-managing teams. On a day-to-day basis, the interaction and behavior of team members is expressed by their conversations. Here, we describe conversations within teams and how these conversations relate to productivity and performance. In addition, team leadership, a critical element in self-management, is described and analyzed. Overall, the story captures the richness of daily life among mature teams and how team activities relate to organizational performance. Much of the material was derived from interviews and observations that were conducted several years after the team system began. Thus, the plant had moved beyond the start-up stage to a more mature phase.

This chapter was written by Henry P. Sims, Jr., and Charles C. Manz.

The Fitzgerald Battery Plant of General Motors uses an innovative and highly effective system of employee self-managing teams to conduct business without bosses. In this chapter, we discuss what actually happens when a serious attempt is made to promote employee participation through self-managing teams. We describe the overall organizational environment and provide some details about the specific roles, structures, procedures, and leadership under which they operate. Most of all, we focus on the people within these teams in order to convey the flavor of their daily interactions. What do they do that makes them different from the traditional production-level employee? What do they talk about? How are their conversations linked to the overall issue of productivity? What is team leadership like? Here, we describe what actually happens.

An important part of the story is the issue of how teams provide self-leadership. There are elected team leaders and external coordinators (facilitators) and no traditional foremen or "bosses." Finally, we discuss how the team system, clearly a success, contributes to the productivity and performance of this remarkable manufacturing system.

THE ORGANIZATIONAL SYSTEM

The Fitzgerald plant, located in rural Fitzgerald, Georgia, was established in 1974 by General Motors Corporation to manufacture sealed maintenance-free automotive batteries. Generally the technology can be described as sequentially interdependent; the output of one team becomes the input of another team. There are small parts production operations and some small assembly operations.

The plant's personnel—about 320—have been organized into teams from the beginning. People at the plant simply use the term "teams"; we classify them as self-managing teams because they meet our definitional criteria. There are three levels of teams. At the top are managers in the *support team*, so named because "we support the people who actually do the work." In the middle is a group of individuals who have technical and operational responsibilities—the *coordinators*. In traditional plants, these employees would be called foremen, general foremen, or technicians, but the role of these coordinators is quite different from the traditional one of foreman. Several of the coordinators have operational responsibility over the manufacturing teams, but this responsibility tends to be more advice and facilitation rather than direction. At the operating level, the employees are organized into approximately 33 operating teams, ranging in size from 3 to about 19 members. People are grouped into teams composed of natural work units that have closely connected, interdependent tasks. Each team has recognizable boundaries, in both physical space and task responsibilities. Products of each team are measured according to input and output, and each team is considered to be a business unto itself. The output of one team becomes the input for other team(s), but the connections among teams are typically buffered by inventories of material between clusters of manufacturing processes.

Wages are based on a pay-for-knowledge concept rather than the traditional pay-for-position principle; that is, employees are paid for what they are *capable* of doing rather than the task they are doing at a particular moment. This system facilitates task flexibility and variety. An employee must demonstrate competence at all jobs on two different teams in order to advance to the highest pay level. This typically takes about two years. One result is high flexibility of response, since most employees can do many types of jobs and they are not financially penalized for short-term assignments to jobs that might command a lower rate in a more traditional pay system. This breadth of job experience, in turn, fosters an unusual appreciation for the "other guy's problems."

The plant's team system features an innovative method for influencing and motivating employee behavior. In addition to the traditional physical production tasks, each team is expected to perform a wide range of responsibilities, many of them traditionally considered to be within the jurisdiction of supervisors or managers. Generally the teams engage in various decision-making and problem-solving activities that focus on production scheduling, process adjustments, product improvement, and, especially, quality problem solving. Teams also deal with internal personnel problems, such as the absenteeism of a team member.

Many of these activities take place during team meetings, which normally serve as problem-solving forums. Each team has at least one half-hour regularly scheduled team meeting per week, and special meetings are called to deal with specific problems. All meetings are held on company time, and employees are paid their regular wage while attending. Meetings are usually conducted by an internally elected team leader. Coordinators or support team members may attend parts of meetings but are not routinely present.

43

TEAM ROLES AND RESPONSIBILITIES

When the plant was started up, an effort was made to involve the teams in at least a portion of roles and responsibilities typically carried out by management at more traditional plants. Because many responsibilities were vested within the teams themselves, traditional foremen or bosses were not needed. Following is a description of how the teams handled responsibilities typically performed by traditional bosses.

Establish relief and break schedules. Teams had great discretion in establishing their own schedules. Since most of the teams were buffered by short-term in-process inventories, they could schedule breaks as they wished. They carried out this role responsibly, often timing breaks to facilitate maintenance or production setup. For example, a short tool or process change might be undertaken while the team was on break.

An effort was made from the very beginning to involve teams in roles and responsibilities typically carried out by management.

Select and dismiss the group leader. Teams elected their own team leader from their membership. Elections were conducted whenever a current leader resigned or was challenged by another team member. (Teams also had the authority to dismiss a team leader, but this was virtually never done. Instead, an ineffective team leader might be encouraged to resign or might be challenged by another.) A few teams had had the same leader since the start-up of the plant; others had had several team leaders over the years.

At first, popular individuals tended to be elected leader; however, teams soon found that the best leaders were those who had organizing, planning, interpersonal, and conflict resolution skills. Eventually so-called popularity diminished as a criterion for election to team leader.

Management appointed coordinators, leaders who were external to the team (although many had served as team leaders). Each coordinator had responsibility for from one to three teams. Although coordinators filled the space in the organizational hierarchy typically occupied by a foreman or general foreman, their role was quite different.

At first, popular individuals tended to be elected team leader. Later, teams elected leaders who had organizing, planning, interpersonal, and conflict resolution skills.

Initiate equipment and machinery repair. Overall, team members tended to make minor repairs themselves in order to keep production flowing. Although major repairs were carried out by the maintenance department, frequently they were initiated by team members. We recall the statement of a team member in a weekly team meeting: "They better get that bearing replaced this weekend, or that machine will break down next week, and we'll lose a day's production!" Most of all, team members seemed to have an unusual degree of ownership in their production equipment; they were very concerned about making the equipment work in the right way.

Make specific job assignments within work group. Each team made its own job assignments. The practices were quite different across teams; one team might rotate jobs every hour, while another would make assignments strictly on a seniority basis. Overall, teams seemed to find a way to satisfy individual member preferences without compromising productivity goals.

Train new members of work group. All teams carried out this responsibility, which is important in terms of developing the wide range of skills required for each new member to advance along the pay scale. Occasionally the external coordinator would pitch in or conduct some special training, and there were more formal training programs for team members.

Ensure that needed production materials and spare parts are available. In many traditional plants, workers allow a production material to deplete in order to take an unauthorized break. At this plant, responsibility to make sure production materials and spare parts were available was vested in the team itself. Team leaders, in particular, spent a great deal of their time ensuring that the materials were available to meet production requirements.

Keep record of hours worked for each group member. The plant had no time clocks. Each team member kept a record of his or her number of hours worked and turned in weekly time records to the team leader and then to the coordinator. When asked, "Don't they cheat?" one team member replied, "Who do they cheat? Other team members! You may be able to get away with it once or twice, but that's all. You can't fool your teammates."

Perform quality control inspections and compile data. For the most part, teams did their own quality inspections and compiled their own quality statistics, typically assigning this responsibility to one member. The plant had no separate quality control inspector, although occasionally, team quality data were audited by a small central quality control department.

Teams did their own quality inspection and compiled quality statistics.

Prepare material and labor budgets. Every year teams undertook a planning exercise in which they prepared a team budget. Budgeting was also done, independently and in parallel, by accountants from the office, and the two proposed budgets were discussed and reconciled in order to arrive at a final budget. Team members required training and appropriate information to carry out this exercise.

Prepare daily log of quantity produced and amount of in-process inventory. For the most part, teams compiled their own in-process inventory records, subject to occasional auditing from production scheduling. Teams knew their own production schedule and kept their own records of how much they produced and the quantity of their in-process inventory.

Recommend engineering changes for equipment, process, and product. As they worked with equipment, teams occasionally requested changes that would lead to significant process or product improvements. One engineer at the division level expressed a preference for placing new or experimental equipment at Fitzgerald. "They *make* it work!" he exclaimed.

Select new members for the group and dismiss members. Teams had considerable discretion over who would join or leave their group. Most intergroup mobility was facilitated by the coordinator, who used interpersonal skills to explore new assignments to different groups. Great effort was made to match the preferences of individuals with teams. Employees would move from one team to another for any of several reasons—for example, to earn a higher pay rate, to perform a different type of work, or to seek more compatible teammates.

Evaluate group members for pay raise. Under the pay-for-knowledge system, an employee had to pass performance tests for all tasks on two different teams to gain the highest pay rate. Performance tests were conducted by a coordinator, team leader, and senior team member.

Conduct safety meetings. Scheduled safety meetings were conducted, normally by the team leader or a coordinator or other technical person. During the early stages of the start-up of the plant, safety performance was poor. Over the years, however, the safety record continuously improved, and by the time of our visits, Fitzgerald's safety performance was in the top quartile of all General Motors plants.

Shut down the process or assembly if quality is wrong. Stop production to solve process or quality problems. Teams had the authority to stop production without asking management permission. Shutdown decisions were made with great discretion and almost always to solve a serious quality or process problem since such a decision might have ramifications for other teams.

Teams had the authority to stop production if quality was wrong.

Conduct weekly group meetings. Teams usually met every week for a half-hour, on company time. In addition, shorter meetings were conducted almost every day, and occasionally a lengthier problem-solving meeting might be conducted to work on special production or quality issues.

Review quarterly performance of company, plant, and group. Each quarter, the plant manager met separately with each team to review company, plant, and team performance. These occasions provided an opportunity for an exchange of communication between the plant manager and team members.

Discipline group members for absenteeism or tardiness. This authority was vested within each team, but not all teams utilized the authority. Coordinators identified this as the most difficult responsibility to get the teams to undertake.

Select new employees for the plant. New employees were selected through an assessment center process. An evaluation team, consisting of one manager, one coordinator, one team leader, and two members of different teams, observed candidates during interpersonal exercises and provided ratings and final judgments.

CONVERSATIONS WITHIN SELF-MANAGING TEAMS

Team meetings proved to be a rich source of information about the culture of the plant. We explored what team members say, what they talk about, whether they deal with serious productivity issues or just fool around, and how their conversation was linked with the operations of the plant. By examining patterns of verbal behavior, we can gain some insight into the culture of the teams at Fitzgerald to discover how they actually conducted business without bosses.

Rewards and Reprimands

Team members frequently exchanged verbal rewards—a compliment, thanks, or praise given in response to an action seen as useful or helpful. Sometimes the exchange was a one-on-one interaction: "Bobby, thanks for helping me with that No. 1 machine last night." At other times, verbal rewards were given in front of the whole team, frequently delivered by the team leader: "We owe a special thanks to Emily for making sure that the materials were ready last Monday. We would have had to shut down if she hadn't looked ahead and gotten what we needed." This category of verbal behavior was particularly important in building team cohesion, cooperation, and esprit de corps. It reinforced helping behavior within teams and promoted the practice of working together to achieve objectives.

The counterpoint to verbal rewards was *verbal reprimands*, by which one team member would direct displeasure or criticism toward one or more fellow team members. (Both positive rewards and criticism were technically designated as "giving feedback." A verbal reprimand was called "negative feedback.") We observed an especially dramatic incident of verbal reprimand at a regular team meeting after several items of routine business were completed. The team leader looked at one of the members and said, "Jerry, we want to talk to you now about your absenteeism." He went on to recount Jerry's record of absenteeism, referring to his record of dates on which Jerry had been absent, and then asked Jerry if he had anything to say about the absenteeism. Jerry briefly mumbled excuses. The team leader continued by describing the effect of his absenteeism on the other team members; the others had to work harder because of Jerry's absences, and the absences were hurting team performance. He called Jerry's absences unacceptable and said, "We won't allow it to continue." One more incident of absenteeism, and Jerry would face a formal disciplinary charge that would be entered into the record. The team leader concluded by asking Jerry about his intentions. Jerry replied, "I guess I've been absent about as much as I can get away with. I guess I better come to work."

The question of team self-discipline is the most controversial.

The question of team self-discipline is the most controversial. Many managers who have not had direct experience with self-managing teams believe that teams are incapable of disciplining their own members. Yet our example shows that self-discipline can take place. We believe that with the proper nurturance, such a disciplinary system can succeed. Indeed, we believe that peer pressure is the most effective form of employee control.

Task Assignments and Work Scheduling

Teams used conversation to carry out the *allocation of task assignments*. Each self-managed team made its own decision of who would perform which job. Some made relatively permanent task assignments on the basis of seniority. Others traded jobs on almost an hour-by-hour basis and still others on a daily or weekly basis, so that each person would have an equal share of both the "dog" jobs and the "gravy" jobs.

This exercise of control over their own tasks had a significant effect on employees' motivation. We sometimes observed employees negotiating with other team members about job allocation. Most of the time, this was handled without substantial conflict, but we observed one incident where emotions ran high. In this case, a six-man team was split across three shifts, and there was a dispute over which shift had the responsibility of completing a particularly dirty and physically demanding job. Finally, the coordinator virtually locked the team members in a room and demanded that they remain there until they worked out a solution. "I could make the decision for them," he told us, "but it will be a better decision, and they will do a better job, if they work it out among themselves."

This incident was atypical for the intensity of the emotions aroused, but it was representative of the way issues were worked out. The usual procedure was to get those involved with a particular problem to sit down and work it out themselves. Hard feelings and bruised egos sometimes resulted, but solutions had a greater chance of enduring because they were agreed upon by the participants themselves and not imposed from the outside.

Many decisions revolved around issues of production scheduling. That is, which specific product should be produced at a particular time? Because of decreasing product demand, this plant had recently undergone a reduction of total production volume but without an employee layoff. One response to this crisis was a significant attempt to reduce in-process inventories. Less inventory also meant less room for mistakes and errors, less flexibility if a particular part was not ready, and, in general, a more intense problem of managing the day-to-day, and even the hour-by-hour, production.

We observed an interesting conversation revolving around this issue. One employee, vigorously complaining about the trouble caused by the lack of buffer inventories, asked why inventories had been cut so low. A fellow team member replied: "Do you know what the cost of interest is these days? For every piece that we have in inventory, we have to pay a finance charge, man! That comes straight out of profits. We have to keep inventories low if our business is going to make a profit!" He was referring to his own team when he used the word "business."

Exercise of control over their own jobs had a significant effect on employees' motivation.

These conversations about production scheduling saved the company a significant amount of money, we believe. In a traditional plant, scheduling would be handled by foremen and general foremen. If a production section ran out of material or parts, it would cease operations until the foreman got the necessary parts. In this plant, shortages severe enough to shut down production were rare because team members were able to anticipate problems and take corrective action in time.

Production Goal Setting and Performance Feedback

The overall plant production goal and schedule is determined by corporate and division requirements, so for the most part, the employees do not participate in setting overall goal levels. Nevertheless, they are very much involved in deciding how these overall levels are to be achieved and are also involved in nonproduction goal setting. One conversation, concerned with making a weekly production quota, began: "We won't have materials to run [product X] on Wednesday. We won't be able to meet our goal this week." A reply: "Why don't we shift over to [product Y] on Wednesday, and build up a bank for next week. We'll be short of [X] this week, but we can get a jump on [Y] for next week, and then we can make up [X] next week." The important factor here is that the team had discretionary authority to shift product mixes within certain time limits, and it used its leeway to overcome short-term difficulties.

Goal setting also occurred in other areas, especially quality and safety. For example, "Our rejection rate last month was 5.8 percent. We need to get it down to below 5 percent for this month. How are we going to do it?" This problem was raised *within* the team and was not an exhortation from a foreman or supervisor.

There was constant feedback. Charts were everywhere.

There was constant feedback to the teams—not only the personal feedback of verbal rewards and reprimands but also daily, weekly, monthly, and quarterly quantitative feedback. Each team maintained charts of quantity, quality, and safety performance. Frequently, we heard reports like, "We made 3,948 units yesterday. We got ahead about 10 percent." Another interesting comment was, "Have you heard about the safety results? The plant is now in the top one-third of the company."

Charts were everywhere. Formal charts posted on walls showed long-term trends in performance. Sloppier informal charts hung on hooks and clipboards and were posted near machines. Feedback was a critical aspect of the information shared at this plant.

Announcements and Problem Resolution

Routine announcements were a part of the team conversations—for example, "The Christmas party will be on Monday. Give George three dollars if you are planning on coming." However, significant amounts of time also were spent on the resolution of *special problems*. One incident revolved around the quality of an in-process product. A young production worker entered the quality control laboratory one afternoon carrying several production pieces. He said to the lab coordinator, "The color just doesn't look right. I'm going to check the chemistry." After doing a quick spot test on the pieces, he announced, "They're out [meaning out of control]. We have to see how much we're in trouble." During the following hour, there was a great deal of scurrying about to assess the extent of the problem, and in the end it was determined that about one-quarter of a day's production of the piece was unacceptable. Adjustments were made to correct the problem and to remove the bad pieces. The worker who noticed the problem stayed two hours beyond his regular quitting time to help find a solution; he was compensated by early time off the next Friday.

This young worker had no special quality control responsibility; he was a production worker within the team that worked on these pieces. He demonstrated significant initiative by spotting the problem early and by *voluntarily* acquiring the technical testing knowledge to make an informed judgment. Later a manager said to us, "You know, it's bad enough when we make a mistake and lose a quarter day's production on those pieces. But think how much more extensive it would have been if he hadn't caught the problem. We probably would have had to scrap several days' production of the full assembly."

In another incident, workers dealt with a quality problem. A meeting had been called by a coordinator to discuss a certain deficiency. Four members from two different teams were present with the coordinator and a quality control technician. The coordinator presented the problem, citing statistics that showed a gradual rise in the reject rate over several weeks. He asked: "What's the problem? What can we do to correct it?" No one had an immediate solution. But the coordinator was patient, and he listened carefully, encouraging workers who spoke. After about five minutes, the meeting seemed to become more productive. Over the next half-hour, several causes of the problem were suggested and several "fixes" proposed. Finally, the group listed the proposed solutions according to ease of implementation and agreed to begin applying them in an attempt to eliminate the problem. Afterward, we asked the coordinator whether he had actually learned anything new or was just going through the motions for the sake of participation. He replied, "I wasn't aware of many of the ideas they brought out. But most of all, they've now taken it on as their problem, and they will do whatever has to be done to solve it."

"It's bad enough when you make a mistake, but think how more extensive it would have been if he hadn't caught the problem."

Both of these examples concerning special problems involved quality issues. Although the self-managing teams were not quality circles, they devoted a significant amount of effort to solving quality problems. Self-managing work groups actually go beyond quality circles. They address quality issues continually, not just during weekly meetings, and are invested with significantly more authority to implement solutions.

Communication Problems

Communication problems dealt with issues between teams as well as within teams. For example, one team might complain about the quality of the product produced earlier in the production process by another team. One solution we saw was the temporary exchange of team members. Working with the other team for a week or so resulted in an improved shared understanding of why particular problems occurred, why certain procedures were important, and how negligence could affect other workers.

Evaluations and Team Membership

Because *performance evaluations for pay raises* were conducted within teams, conversations addressed this issue. For example in a team meeting, a member said to the team leader: "How about running a performance test on the [Z] machine? I think I'm ready." The reply was, "O.K. I'll try to schedule it this week."

Teams also talked about *entry to and exit from the team.* We attempted to determine rules for assignment of employees to teams but never discerned any. A typical answer was, "Well, we just work it out." One team meeting we observed addressed this issue. Because of lower production levels, this team had been asked to reduce its numbers by one person, who would be assigned to a temporary construction team that was being formed to undertake repair and cleanup work. The team leader presented the decision issue to the group and asked, "How should we handle it?" The first reply was, "Well, unless someone wants to go, we should do it by seniority." The man with the least seniority then spoke up: "Well, that's me, and I don't want to go." The team leader asked, "Does anyone want to go?" One person asked, "Would they be working outside? Is there any carpentry work?" Eventually this person volunteered to move to the construction team. He wanted to be outside and to do some craft work.

TEAM LEADERSHIP

The Fitzgerald plant's external work team leaders are called coordinators. Coordinators are in a hierarchical position that would be occupied by foremen and general foremen—that is, "bosses"—in a more traditional production plant.

Often there is confusion surrounding the responsibilities of a coordinator in a team system. He or she is positioned over and is responsible for work groups that are deliberately intended to be self-managing, an inherent contradiction. The question, "How does one lead employees who are supposed to lead themselves?" represents this dilemma. To add confusion to this leader role, Fitzgerald's work groups also contain a within-group team leader, who is a member of and elected by the group.

What do "coordinators" do? What are the behaviors and actions of effective coordinators? If employee work teams are supposed to be "participative," or "self-managing," then why are coordinators necessary?

Traditional leadership theory does not apply to the unique situation of participative or self-managing teams. The traditional concept is that the appointed leader is a legitimate authority figure and therefore acts like a "boss." With self-managing teams, however, this fundamental assumption is largely rejected. External leaders of self-managing work groups do not use the traditional legitimate authority and do not act as a boss. In this situation, what type of leader behavior is most appropriate when traditional assumptions about power, authority, and influence are challenged? To what extent should coordinators give directions, assign tasks, evaluate performance, and dispense rewards and reprimand as traditional bosses typically do? To what extent should they act as a facilitator and communicator who typically does not invoke direct authority over the work team? Who makes the myriad of decisions that are necessary to carry out the daily tasks of the group? Further, how does the role of the external leader differ from the role of leaders who emerge from within the team? Finally, what are the behaviors that differentiate effective leaders?

How does one lead employees who are supposed to lead themselves?

The coordinators are jointly selected by management and by the coordinator team. Many are former team leaders; others are selected because of some technical ability. Most do not have a college degree. The pay level of coordinators is roughly equivalent to foremen and general foremen in more traditional plants. Each team is assigned to a coordinator, who may have responsibility for one to three teams.

There are no formal guidelines regarding a coordinator's duties; rather, coordinator behaviors seem to be loosely defined according to social convention rather than any structured set of rules and regulations.

Role of the Coordinator

Our inquiry into the role of the coordinator was intended to answer the question, "What important behaviors can coordinators use in their work?" We first posed this question to upper plant management and elicited the following answers (listed in order of importance):

1. Try to get a team to solve a problem on its own.
2. Help a team solve conflict within its group.
3. Tell people (teams and individuals) when they do something well.
4. Tell the truth even when it may be disagreeable or painful.
5. Encourage team members to discuss problems openly.
6. Asks for a solution to a problem rather than proposing (or telling) a solution. People promote what they create.
7. Encourage teams to set performance goals.
8. Provide teams with the information they need to run their business.
9. Anticipate future problems or situations (planning).
10. Encourage team self-evaluation.
11. Train teams in the philosophy of the plant.
12. Be a resource to a team.

The list provides some interesting insights. First, several of the behaviors, including the behavior obtaining the highest importance, reveal an emphasis on getting teams to manage their own efforts (for example, behaviors 1, 6, and 7). We also noted this emphasis on passing control to work teams during our numerous observations at the plant. Coordinators often purposely avoided providing answers or direction to employees even when they possessed the ability to do so, at times, to the extent of frustrating the workers. In one instance, an employee ran into a problem when welding a guardrail on a ramp and asked the coordinator what he should do. The coordinator responded by asking the worker what he thought he should do. The employee thought a moment, provided his opinion, and proceeded to act on it.

Another major theme of the behaviors is a focus on some form of communication (for example, behaviors 3, 4, 5). Observations indicated that communication—a coordinator's direct communication with team members, as well as efforts to facilitate communication within and between teams—is crucial, and most coordinators realized the importance, sometimes facilitating temporary exchanges of members between teams in order to improve interteam communications. Problems observed on the plant floor and discussed during team meetings often pointed to communication as both a cause and potential cure.

Finally, several behaviors indicated directly what many of the behaviors discussed so far have suggested indirectly: a coordinator should be a facilitator (behaviors 2 and 8). For example, in the incident already noted, employees asked a coordinator to make a decision and resolve a conflict over who should do a particularly unpleasant job. Instead of making the decision, the coordinator facilitated an energetic conflict resolution meeting that helped the team to make its own decision.

Several behaviors reveal an emphasis on getting teams to manage their own efforts.

We also asked the elected team leaders to identify important behaviors for coordinators to use in their work and got the following replies:

1. Ask for solutions to problems.
2. Be a resource to a team (concerning both technical and personnel problems).
3. Create an atmosphere of mutual trust and understanding between the coordinator and the team and within the team.
4. Provide honest feedback.
5. Communicate production schedule changes to teams.
6. Arrange problem solving and present possible solutions.

7. Get tooling, supplies, and materials for a team.

8. Provide backing and communication to the team leader.

9. Learn details about team operations.

10. Provide information to a team to solve its problems.

11. Help with interteam problem solving concerning quality control.

12. Try to get team to set performance goals.

13. Recheck production schedule and inventory.

14. Help in the maintenance of equipment (e.g., get parts, needed personnel).

15. Support the team leader in the support group.

16. Communicate a problem solution of one team to another team that can help.

17. Keep abreast of new machines and processes (innovation).

18. Encourage a team to solve its own problems.

19. Maintain good communication between coordinators (to coordinate efforts throughout the plant).

20. Keep the team leader in the chain of communication.

21. Encourage a team to evaluate itself.

Team leaders seem to place especially high importance on the facilitative role as opposed to a directive role of coordinators. The two top-ranked behaviors support this interpretation.

Observations generally support the importance that team leaders place on the coordinator's facilitative behavior and their apparent dislike of external direction. Views obtained from team members through discussion and observations (including those of team leaders) indicated that they often wished to be left to do their work on their own and solve their own problems. In fact, it was generally understood that teams resented overly directive coordinator behavior.

One team meeting we observed was convened and run by a team to solve an urgent quality problem. The coordinator and manager from the support group who were present served only as information resources. In another case, however, we observed a coordinator get impatient with the team's progress in solving a problem. Consequently, he essentially took charge and dictated a course of action to the team. Prior to his intervention, the team members were interested and highly involved in problem solving. The subsequent tone of the meeting, however, reflected their low interest and irritation. We thought that implementation would surely suffer because of this overly directive coordinator. At the same time, however, some teams left totally on their own to solve problems became frustrated and dissatisfied with difficult situations in which a coordinator provided what they believed was inadequate direction. We concluded that there is a fine line between overdirection and underdirection on the part of coordinators. Team members placed a high value on independence to manage themselves, but sometimes they needed—and wanted—guidance and assistance. Coordinators must make a decision regarding the appropriate level of involvement based on each situation.

There is a fine line between overdirection and underdirection.

A second pattern of responses from team leaders concerns the degree of honesty and truthfulness with which coordinators deal with work groups. The suggested coordinator behaviors "create an atmosphere of mutual trust and understanding" and "provide honest feedback" reflect this type of behavior. Again observations supported this view. One team distrusted and disliked a particular coordinator who apparently had presented a work team's position to upper management differently from the way in which he had led the group to believe that he would. Both individual discussions with team members and observations of weekly team meetings indicated the strong value placed on having a coordinator whom the team could count on and trust.

The Paradox of Team Leadership

At Fitzgerald, there sometimes seems to be a contradiction between semantics and reality. The teams are regarded to be self-managing. Yet we are exploring and discussing the role of an appointed external leader to these groups. The essence of this dilemma can be captured by the question: If these groups are supposed to be self-managing, then why is an external leader needed at all?

First, upper plant management saw the coordinator's role as that of a facilitator to help work teams manage themselves. By facilitating problem solving of team members and communication throughout the work system, coordinators can help to ensure that teams are working properly.

The social skills of the coordinator seem to be much more critical than technical expertise to successful performance.

Team leaders see the coordinator's job as a balance between a facilitator who does not interfere with group functioning and a resource to provide some direction, a precarious position for coordinators. They must take action when needed but be essentially a backdrop for the team's activities when they are not needed. According to team leaders truthfulness and trustworthiness are important characteristics for coordinators to possess in carrying out this role.

The ultimate question is what sort of expertise the coordinators should have in this type of work organization. While technical expertise is useful and appropriate (especially to establish baseline credibility), the social skills of the coordinator seem to be much more critical. In many ways, the coordinator acts as a counselor and a communication facilitator. Perhaps the most frequent type of coordinator verbal behavior that we heard was the reflective question, throwing the burden of judgment and decision back on the team leader or team member. Coordinators become applied day-by-day "organizational development" specialists, spending a significant amount of their time facilitating the capabilities of a team to manage itself.

The most frequent coordinator verbal behavior was the reflective question.

Overall, it appears that a new and sensitive role is prescribed for leaders of the self-managing. It is a role that may initially cause uneasiness in its performers and inadvertently prompt a search for concrete tasks when compared to more traditional supervisory positions. The effective coordinator may be primarily a facilitator who relies heavily on communication and who carefully balances a hands–off and a directive style according to the requirements of each unique situation. In our previous book, *SuperLeadership*, and, in the final chapter of this book, we explore this issue in more detail.

THE CONNECTION BETWEEN TEAMS AND PRODUCTIVITY

Our investigation into team roles and leadership yielded rich evidence of both attitudes and behavior in the Fitzgerald plant. The conversations were particularly enlightening. While verbal behavior inevitably reflected some amount of self-concern and was sometimes trivial, the organizational commitment and motivation of these employees were among the highest we have ever observed.

What was the connection between teams and the high level of motivation and commitment? How do team conversations and behavior get translated into bottom–line productivity results?

First, we should ask whether this plant was considered to be effective. Specific data are proprietary, but we did have access to internal data that showed good performance. At the bottom line, it had demonstrated the capability to produce products at a cost significantly lower than similar plants of traditional management style. The turnover at the plant has been extremely low. One manager listed on the fingers of one hand the people who had voluntarily resigned. Finally, overall attitude survey results showed that the levels of satisfaction in the plant were among the highest in the entire company, exceeding even those of many white-collar groups. Most important, many prominent people whom we talked to in the corporation regarded the innovative work structure at the plant as a success. This success has sustained itself over several years and through the transition of several plant managers. (General Motors is now attempting to extrapolate and apply throughout the corporation the lessons learned from this plant, although this issue of diffusion is another story and is not without controversy. Perhaps the success with the Saturn venture is a preliminary indication that General Motors has made some significant progress.)

This plant produced products at a cost significantly lower than traditionally managed plants.

Once we assume productivity success, the next question focuses on the connection between teams and productivity. What is there about the roles teams assume and what team members say that gets translated into bottom-line results? Why is talk more than just talk? Part of the reason that conversations get turned into productivity is *information sharing*, and part is influence on employee *motivation*.

Information Sharing

Ask any executive what his or her major problem is, and the chances are good that the reply would be something like: "Communication. Our communication is not what it should be. We just never seem to have the right information at the right place at the right time." Inadequate communication often means inadequate information sharing. More often than not, this problem is the result of a policy of secrecy: tell employees only what they need to know to do their jobs. But there frequently is a significant difference between what a manager *thinks* an employee needs to know and what the employee *actually* needs to know. The result is that the employee often lacks the optimal information needed to perform the job.

At Fitzgerald, management shared virtually all information that was not considered personal. The guiding belief was that only the individual employee and the team itself, not management, were in a position to know just which information was important. The net result was a climate of openness that we found virtually unprecedented in our previous experience. Furthermore, this information sharing provided a basis for employees to engage in *proactive* problem solving; they did not need to wait for management to present a problem for solution, instead discovering and correcting problems at a relatively early stage.

Individual Motivation

Conversations also seemed to influence productivity through their influence on individual motivation. Over and over again, we observed individual behavior affecting the team. If an individual performed well, the team as a whole was seen to be the beneficiary; on the other hand, when an individual fell down, the group was seen to be hurt. The net result was strong peer pressure to contribute to the efforts and performance of the team. Motivation and discipline came from within the team, not from management. This motivation and peer pressure were manifested mainly through group conversations.

The important point is that management's role did not seem to be to provide motivation and discipline directly to individual employees, as is the case in traditional plants. Instead, management created a climate in which motivation and discipline came mainly from within the individual employee and from fellow employees. In our opinion, this is the most effective form of motivation, and it translates into bottom-line productivity. People who wish to perform well and achieve are more likely to do so with the team system. Conversations within work teams are the means by which interpersonal influence is translated into motivation and, ultimately, bottom-line results.

Management created a climate in which discipline came mainly from within.

We do not wish to leave the impression that the plant was a model of tranquility and harmony. On the contrary, the members of the self-managing teams were tough and intense. We observed emotional conflict, but the prevailing mode seemed to be to deal with the conflict openly and directly. Overall, the level of motivation and commitment was high.

IMPLICATIONS FOR BUSINESS
WITHOUT BOSSES

Fitzgerald is a provocative example of how teams can serve to conduct business without bosses. The Fitzgerald teams illustrate the potential of people to work together in teams to achieve high standards of quality and productivity. At Fitzgerald, the teams do it *without* bosses. A point to emphasize is that this plant is not a Japanese operation so we do not have the difficulty of sorting out the differential effects of culture versus managerial organization and style. From evidence available at this plant, it is clear that American workers can respond responsibly and productively to participative programs. Listen to their day-to-day conversations; the message of their competence and commitment comes through loud and clear.

The Fitzgerald story can be helpful in bringing to the surface reservations and fears about empowering workers. It provides powerful arguments in favor of the notions that teams can be extremely effective under the right conditions.

Key Lessons for Creating Business Without Bosses

1. Encourage and help employees to solve their own problems. The increased ownership and commitment that results can pay off handsomely in terms of improved performance.
2. Give teams responsibility for a wide range of roles and functions, many of them traditionally considered managers' work. If they are provided with the training, information, equipment, materials, and, especially, the opportunity, they can accomplish significant work.
3. Leaders in self-managing team systems, especially those outside the team, need to learn a new, challenging role that carefully balances guidance and direction. Often asking the right questions is more important than giving answers.
4. Mature self-managing teams can be a significant source of organizational competitiveness, as well as satisfaction, for the work force.

Chapter 3

The Good and the Bad of Teams: A Practical Look at Successes and Challenges

In some industries the pursuit of business without bosses through teams is a proved competitive strategy. One executive in the company described in this chapter explained the strong commitment to teams simply: "We wanted a state-of-the-art social system to go with [our] state-of-the-art technology." This chapter tells the story of what has been described as the most successful start-up in the history of the paper industry. But teams are not a magic cure-all. The story reveals the difficult challenges of moving toward business without bosses through teams, as well as some significant payoffs. Teams have helped to produce scores of motivated employees, efficiency, and financial success. Yet team managers have struggled with their new confusing and threatening role. Some employees have felt like losers. For others, progress has been frustratingly slow. Despite these challenges, this story demonstrates the capacity of teams to succeed.

This chapter was written by Charles C. Manz and John Newstrom.

This chapter is about the start-up of self-managing teams in the pursuit of business without bosses in a paper mill. Papermaking is an industry in which self-managing teams are rapidly becoming the norm, at least among new start-ups. The focus here is on Lake Superior Paper Co., which began operation in late 1987 as a joint venture of a large American corporation previously involved in mill management and a major regional electrical power company. Our study of the mill occurred during its second year. The new mill is located in Duluth, Minnesota, near plentiful timber sources, is not unionized, and is already the largest producer of uncoated, super-calendared (glossy paper used in magazines, newspaper supplements, catalogs, etc.) ground wood paper in North America. The mill is equipped with state-of-the-art technology and is designed to produce nearly a quarter-million tons of paper a year. It is a highly automated facility, with operations continuously monitored by skilled workers.

The mill has several relatively distinct operations: receiving, washing, cutting, and debarking large wood logs; grinding the logs into refined pulp; converting the pulp to long, continuous sheets of paper; ironing and polishing the sheets to create the glossy finish; rewinding the paper and cutting it to desired sizes; wrapping and warehousing paper rolls; and using biodegradable by-products to fuel the steam plant that powers the mill's operations. Workers in the mill are organized into over 20 teams, among them, the wood yard crew, wood handling operation, pulp mill, paper machine, calendaring and roll finishing, laboratory, and maintenance areas on multiple work shifts. There is also a core of team managers in the plant and a design team (consisting of the president and vice-presidents) that spearheaded the initial mill design, start-up, and task assignments.

A self-managing team system was chosen for the new mill, said one of the mill managers, because "it would have been against the norm in the paper industry if we used a traditional work system in a new start-up operation." According to the vice-president for human resources, traditional management systems are not common at all in newer mills. "All of the last 10 paper mills built in the United States use some form of participative/sociotechnical system program," he added. Another executive explained, "We had a state-of-the-art mill in terms of technology. We wanted a state-of-the-art social system to go with it, not an old outdated kind of traditional system."

Clearly, a newly emerging tradition in the industry was a major driver in the decision to go to teams. "We wanted a state-of-the-art social system to go with the technology."

In the early stages of the mill's start-up and operation, all levels of management provided specific direction to the work teams. The mill managers typically had significant technical experience, while the majority of the workers had no prior experience in the paper industry. Thus, most actions in the start-up stages were intended to emphasize the technical aspects of the mill. Proper technical functioning (focused on the papermaking process, machines and equipment, computer systems, and materials) was seen as the primary avenue through which the mill could get off the ground and reach profitability at an early stage. Movement toward self-managing teams (doing business without bosses) was expected to progress continuously but only as the teams and their members matured in both technical and social skills. The social system, in particular, required development and refinement of roles; mission, goal, and value statements; reward systems; career development procedures; justice systems; behavioral norms; and selection/placement mechanisms.

Because of the enormity of such tasks, each team still has a manager who is directly responsible for its supervision and support. As the teams mature, the direct role of these managers will gradually fade into the background, and they will assume different responsibilities, revolving around project assignments.

The development of truly self-managing teams was expected to take from five to eight years. Initially, teams were under the direct leadership of the team manager with no rotation of member skill roles and responsibilities; ultimately, self-managing teams will have the requisite skills and abilities within the team, with members exercising control over their problems and rotating among various coordinating and scheduling roles. Figure 3.1 depicts the long-term evolutionary plan, with team managers moving from direct supervision (stage 1), to positions of shared authority (stage 2), to boundary managers and leaders (stages 3 and 4).

STAGE 1: START-UP TEAM

Authority
Expert
Teacher
Problem solver
Coordinator
Team supervisor
Mentor

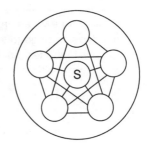

STAGE 2: TRANSITIONAL TEAM

Shared authority
Monitor
Helper
Example setter
Teacher
Evaluator
Information provider
Link to other teams

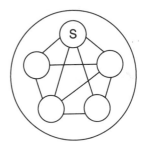

STAGE 3: WELL-TRAINED, EXPERIENCED TEAM

Manager of boundary
Auditor
Expert
Resource provider
Goal setting guider
Information provider
Protector/buffer

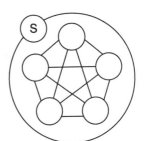

STAGE 4: WELL-TRAINED, MATURE TEAM

Boundary leader
Shared values
Coach
Champion
Counselor
Resource provider
Supporter
Shared responsibilities

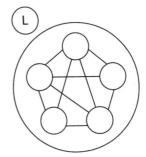

Figure 3.1. Evolution of the team leader's role. *S* = supervisor or manager; *L* = leader.

After a year of operation, a company executive asserted that the mill had achieved "the most successful start-up in the paper industry's history and is already outproducing the best paper makers in the world." Key performance indicators of average efficiency, speed, tonnage, job lot percentage, and waste were more favorable than original (and even revised) forecasts based on comparative information from other mill start-ups. The mill even became profitable in its first year, unusual in the paper industry, where the art of papermaking entails a relatively slow learning curve for employee operators.

Company executives attributed the favorable early results to a combination of factors: state-of-the-art technology, quality of the work force hired (both its overall work ethic and high average level of education), and the self-managing team system. In fact, a common view, expressed by management and workers alike, was that without the team system, the achievement level of the operation would be significantly behind where it is today.

We discussed the work system in detail with many workers from many teams in the mill. We talked with employees, team managers, and design team executives. They told us about their experiences in the mill, their reactions, specific results, problem areas, and feelings about both team managers and the entire organization. They also discussed changes they desired to see take place in the young enterprise.

Without the self-managing team system, the achievement level of the operation would be significantly behind where it is today.

We also reviewed company documents, covering descriptions of the design team plan, the organization's sociotechnical plan for improving productivity and quality of work/life, the team training process, the orientation program, and the demonstrated performance system (compensation based on certified skills). We toured the physical facility at several stages in the mill's development, and we were informally briefed by members of the human resources staff.

Ultimately, we came up with a series of conclusions that we sorted into two primary areas: themes contributing to success and remaining problems. From our examination of both the successes and struggles experienced in these groups, we derived useful lessons for self-managing teams.

THEMES UNDERLYING SUCCESS

Emphasize the technical side first for a smoother start-up. One of the most striking features in the mill's successful start-up was its strategy to focus on the one initial most critical element for short-term survival and success: attaining satisfactory levels of production. One member of management explained, "Initial emphasis on the technical side helped the mill avoid the frequently typical performance dip [productivity below expected levels in comparison to more traditional operations] experienced in most self-managing team start-ups." Frequently, a new self-managing team system requires time to work out enough operations bugs and to allow workers and managers to adjust to employee self-management. Consequently, in the early stages of start-up, an emphasis on the social or employee self-management side of the operation can cause the overall work system (including both the technical and social components) to underperform more traditional systems. This additional pressure requires considerable patience and commitment from the organization's management, even causing some to abandon the system before it has had a chance to mature and prove itself.

This mill experienced no initial performance dip, largely, we believe, due to the strong commitment to refining the technical aspects of the system first. Extensive time and effort were devoted to facilitating the teams' technical skills, which meant that the highly experienced managers stayed directly involved in daily operations (consistent with stage 1 in Figure 3.1). Also important in the mill's early success was the decision to hire a significant number of workers (approximately 25 percent of the mill's work force) who had prior technical experience in other papermaking operations. With this infusion of relevant backgrounds and expertise, a basic level of technical competence prevailed in the mill from its inception.

The social aspects of the system, on the other hand, were designed (and expected) to mature more slowly. The formal target was to achieve mature self-managing teams in about five years, with a gradual transition across the four stages portrayed in Figure 3.1. In our interviews, most workers acknowledged that the evolution of highly mature teams would be slow, although almost all employees believed that their teams were slightly ahead of scheduled development (most members as well as team managers perceived that they were already in at least stage 2). There were also hints at some discomfort with the imbalance between the mill's stronger progress on the technical versus the social dimension. (One worker commented, "There is a myth here that we have balanced our social growth with our technical growth.") This impatience, we sensed, may have been partially due to two factors. First, the workers may believe that because they had attained early technical goals so readily, they should be able to accomplish the same dramatic results in the social domain. Second, we suspect that many workers are unaccustomed to thinking about their work in five-year developmental time frames. Consequently, they may implicitly abbreviate the team-maturity time line for their own teams.

Introducing self-managing teams into a greenfield site is easier than at an established site. Another cause of the predicted performance dip occurring in many self-managing team experiments is the difficulty that employees have in adjusting to new expectations and modes of interaction when a dramatic shift from one work design to another occurs. Since the mill we studied was new (a greenfield site) and many employees were new to the labor force, the majority of employees were not required to adjust to an internal transition to a new technological system or to a new set of social relationships. The experienced technicians, in contrast, had to make a significant adjustment relative to their past work experiences.

All job applicants were rigorously screened in the hiring process to provide reasonable assurance that they would support the idea of self-managing teams. In addition, an extensive orientation process carefully exposed all new employees to the philosophy and operations of socio-technical systems. Thus, the entire system was predisposed toward successful implementation, in contrast to other organizational change efforts where unlearning, as well as new learning, must take place.

Real participation leads to satisfaction and commitment for most employees. Some of the most dramatic clues to the self-managing team system's impact on the mill's work force were expressed in comments made by team members. One said simply, "I like to go to work here," with another adding that "They [mill management] treat you like real people." Even when workers expressed frustration with some aspects of the mill's operation (e.g., the unusually high number of meetings or management's reluctance to hire short-term staff to meet temporary work demands during start-up so as to avoid future layoffs), the comments were usually softened by modifications such as, "But here we have the power to do something about it."

Indications of employee commitment to the organization (or, at least, a low level of desire to leave) as a product of participative orientation were reflected time and again in comments indicating that "I wouldn't work anywhere else." In fact, many workers stated that they had serious doubts about whether they would ever be able to work in a more traditional, authority-based system again because of the wasted human abilities they had witnessed and experienced. Employees related the story of a former co-worker who had relocated to another city; he had started a new job but just a few months later was seeking new employment. The clear reason given was that he could no longer tolerate an authoritarian style of management.

"Here we have the power to do something about it" (the frustrating aspects of the mill).

The employees we interviewed perceived that the participative work system was producing positive results in terms of their own quality of work life (as well as achieving efficiency, early profitability, very low turnover, and almost negligible absenteeism). They found company-related social functions like picnics fun to attend because people got along so well. The common feeling was that team managers were not opponents of workers but "more like team members." A pervasive sense of trust in and respect for the mill's top management team was conveyed, with one employee explaining that "they do everything they promise they will do." Weekly team meetings were seen as a useful process for cementing social relationships and opening up communication lines.

Finally, the participative selection process (team members are directly involved in selecting new employees) used to staff the mill provided a powerful sense of ownership for the work force. Since any member of the interview team could, with adequate justification, veto any applicant he or she believed should not be hired, "It inflates your ego to have that kind of power," explained one employee with obvious pride.

Employee learning contributes to constructive empowerment. The paper mill appears to have established a generally favorable climate for employee learning and development. Workers are given a substantially wider range of responsibilities than in traditional manufacturing settings, typically working on multiple job assignments derived from work allocation decisions from within the team. Members also make many decisions and perform several functions that have traditionally been in the domain of management. Consequently, learning new skills is critically important in this mill.

Concurrent with the timing of our interviews, a pay-for-knowledge/skill system (officially known as the demonstrated performance system) was being developed. This system was designed to provide employees with the opportunity (and to encourage them) to cross-train in a wide range of job functions (skill blocks) both within and across mill teams. When employees believe they are ready to be certified as capable on a new skill block, they are tested in order to assess whether they have the adequate knowledge, can apply the skill effectively, and get results. As skill blocks are added to an employee's repertoire, he or she receives advanced technical ratings resulting in salary base increments ranging as high as 22 percent for each advancement in grade.

The introduction of this pay system sent a powerful message to the work force that learning is needed, expected, and integral to the long-term success of the mill. The pay increments were clearly attractive to the employees we interviewed, but they also seemed to value intrinsically the opportunity to improve themselves and help the organization. One worker explained, "I like the idea of pay increases, but I also just plain like to learn."

This theme—a positive emphasis on learning—was echoed by several team members and managers. One team manager explained that the workers "are learning much quicker because they are being allowed to learn." Another added that "the mill would be years behind schedule" if it was based on a traditional system. The organization's emphasis on learning was best exemplified by one of the team manager's transitional roles, the teacher. One manager summed up his primary role at this time as to "first teach and then allow them [the workers] to do."

In effect, empowering workers in this mill involves more than just giving them more responsibility and involvement in decisions. It is also aggressively helping them to acquire the skills and knowledge to contribute successfully.

PROBLEMS REMAINING TO BE RESOLVED

Reactions to the concept of self-managing teams often range from complete skepticism to their embracement as a cure-all. This diversity of responses may stem from a variety of reasons—ignorance of the approach, philosophical differences, biased or unsubstantiated reporting, or unique (idiosyncratic) experiences with it. Actual results with teams appear to fall somewhere between the two extreme possibilities of unmitigated success or total failure. Although some half-hearted and misguided attempts have clearly failed, some successful applications have also occurred. But even the road to success is often filled with roadblocks and other obstacles, and this is true of this mill's experience as well.

Lake Superior Paper has clearly been successful through its early stages of operation, from both a technical and a social perspective. Nevertheless, many significant challenges remain, and this reality seemed to be recognized by mill employees at all levels.

Support for Team Managers in Their New Role

Supervisory positions historically have been fraught with conflict; supervisors are often caught in the middle, trying to satisfy the demands of management from above and expectations of workers from below in the organizational hierarchy. Team managers in the paper mill are no different. One manager described her primary role as a kind of buffer that "gets it from both ways," resulting in the occasional wish that she could just turn toward one group or the other and say, "All right, you do it."

Self-managing teams present additional challenges that make the team manager's role even more difficult. First, many of the managers obtained their work and supervisory experiences in more traditional organizations, where directive modes of leadership were the norm. The transition to a team system calls for not only a new set of roles but an entirely different managerial philosophy for the treatment of employees. Clearly this can create internal conflict for team leaders. Second, there is a clear organizational plan for the evolution of team leader roles from start-up mode to those ultimately required for supporting a well-trained, mature team (see Figure 3.1). Consequently, the team leaders are, and will continue to be, in a constant state of role flux. The issue is compounded by the fact that some teams in the mill are progressing at different speeds on their own paths to maturity. Therefore, the roles required of team managers are somewhat different across teams within the mill.

Third, many of the mill's employees were drawn from work backgrounds in traditionally managed firms. Therefore, initially, they lacked unreserved trust in the new system and also required development of social (teamwork) skills. These circumstances provided additional challenges for team managers.

Finally, there is a haunting, if not always stated, fear among some of the team managers that they risk managing themselves out of a job. If they were to be truly successful, their team would become self-managing and appear not to require a team manager any longer.[1]

In general, however, the team managers seemed to value their new roles despite the many challenges. A manager who had previously worked in a more traditional mill for 12 years explained, "I could never go back. I saw all that wasted potential there. Here, if you ask if someone will do something, you get three people stuck in the door volunteering for it. They're really gung-ho." Other team managers supported this view with their comments. Although they had little difficulty identifying flaws in the system (e.g., dealing with a dozen different opinions from team members all at once; unrealistic expectations from employees regarding their own rate of advancement through the skill blocks), most of them expressed significant satisfaction with their positions.

I could never go back. I saw all that wasted potential."

Other issues also came forth from the team managers. One explained, "Technical operations in the mill are a piece of cake, but developing the team will keep you awake at night." Some of the specific issues they faced in team development included the frustration of waiting for the team to come up with its own solution to a problem (while the team manager withholds a solution in order to facilitate the team's growth), being "kind of a psychologist" so as to pay attention to workers' feeling and needs, and ensuring that team members are not too tough in managing themselves (a rather unique situation). For example, if a team member fails to pull his or her weight on the team (e.g., is chronically absent), the manager may have to "take the (figurative) lynching rope out of their hands" (a rich metaphor offered by one team leader) and try to fashion a peaceful settlement rather than mete out the more traditional punishment.

Aside from intrateam challenges, the team managers were most concerned with the ambiguity surrounding their own future roles. The pervasiveness of this uncertainty was exemplified by one team member's flat assertion: "We know our team manager won't be there forever. Eventually we intend to phase him out, and then we'll be managing on our own." Despite strong upper management assurances that the team managers will eventually shift their focus to special projects and boundary leadership functions, the message had not yet sunk in. It was not clear whether it was simply the ambiguity inherent in what would eventually constitute their new leadership role or the lack of job security that concerned them the most.

One clue to the depth of their worry came from the positive anticipation with which they viewed the mill's possible expansion in the near future. Team managers realized that new teams of workers would need a new set of team managers. If they were successful in moving their existing teams through the first two or three stages of team development, they might be able to bypass the uncertainty of struggling with stage 4 team leadership roles by being selected for team management positions in the new section of the mill. This revealed a curious irony: After doing their job well and struggling through the reportedly sleepless nights of developing strong and independent teams, they looked forward to going back and starting over again. (Note that this would mean going back to a stage that required stronger leader directiveness.)

Despite strong assurances that the team managers would simply shift their focus to special projects, the message had not yet sunk in.

Emerging Feelings of Inequity for Employees Who See Themselves as "Losers"

Most organizations have employee groups who perceive that they are disadvantaged at one time or another. Lake Superior Paper Company was no different. Certainly this is true of the team managers, who perceive the possible loss of their jobs as the teams mature. But they are not the only ones who sense that they are being treated unfairly. The most notable class of paper mill employee who appeared vulnerable to perceptions of loss were those who were hired specifically because they possessed considerable prior technical experience in the paper industry; we refer to them as "techs." To expedite the technical start-up of the mill, the managerial design team hired a substantial number of employees with papermaking expertise. The use of these techs clearly expedited the start-up from an operational perspective, but it also produced some disadvantages. First, many of the techs came from more traditional work systems and faced not only the problems of mill start-up but also adaptation to a sharply different social system and an unlearning of prior attitudes. Movement for the techs along the path toward trusting the new form of management was slower. One inexperienced worker noted that the techs still displayed a lot of skepticism, clung to previous mill traditions, and expressed a lot of reservations ("I'll believe it when I see it").

The techs' feeling of inequity stemmed from two sources: performance of tasks that they viewed as beneath their status (and this offended their dignity) and the more rapid acquisition of increased status (and income) by other, inexperienced workers. As the inexperienced workers progressed and learned and performed higher-skill and higher-status jobs, this meant that the techs, who were hired at level 7 of the nine-point pay scale, increasingly had to perform a variety of lower-status jobs (like hosing down the floor). They would have escaped such menial chores in a more traditional system with narrowly defined job tasks for each level. Additionally, under the demonstrated performance pay system in the new mill, they would soon (within 18 months) be required to acquire the knowledge and demonstrate the skills consistent with the 7 level of pay (e.g., learn an entire process and be able to function anywhere within it) regardless of their previous background and experience. To some, this appeared to be a regressive step.

Unlearning prior attitudes was required.

Even more visible than loss of status was the techs perception of inequity in terms of financial rewards. Although they started at a salary level roughly double that of the inexperienced workers, the latter group was in a position to receive much larger relative, and absolute, increases in salary as they became certified on new skill blocks. The techs foresaw the day (probably several years away) when newer employees would catch up to their own salaries and match their status from an earnings and expertise perspective. Although the techs would be losing nothing in the process, it was hard for them to watch others gain more.

When our interviews touched upon the pay-for-knowledge/skill system that was being phased into the mill, reaction of the employees indicated that this was a controversial topic. (The pay system provides increases in worker pay contingent on learning and being certified on multiple jobs, or essentially more pay for more job knowledge.) "You've hit a raw nerve there," was the representative response of one employee. Inexperienced employees viewed the certification process very favorably ("I like to learn, and the money is motivating for me, too"); the techs seemed almost unanimously opposed to it. (Progression from their current level to the top of the salary scale, two steps away, would bring about only a 5 percent salary gain for them.) This created a powerful dilemma for mill management; the pay system was viewed as integral to the mill's progress toward self-management yet created perceptions of winners and losers. To the credit of mill management, the salary scale was revised to allow a two-step gain amounting to over 18 percent.

Impatience with Slow Development

The evolution and development of mature self-managing teams are not smooth processes, despite occasional claims of instant success. On the contrary, unrealistic expectations or simplistic assumptions that the achievements of teams can be quick and painless can sabotage the long-term chances of success. The demands and rewards can be great for members and leaders alike, but if the participants are not emotionally prepared, patient, organizationally supported, and carefully trained for the challenges, disillusionment is a real danger. (This may represent an especially serious obstacle in countries whose cultures have not traditionally prepared first-level employees to assume significant self-management responsibilities.)

Lake Superior Paper Company did not escape the frustrations surrounding the pace of change, the demands made on workers, the time frame required for maturation of teams, and the fragility inherent in intrateam (and interteam) relationships. Mill employees had been carefully informed that progress toward team development requires time, patience, and hard work, but differing perceptions of the actual and desired pace of change nevertheless resulted in some frustrations. Some workers indicated that "we're moving too fast . . . I feel like we're on a runaway train." Almost all expressed concern over the number of meetings to attend. "I've got a meeting before and after my shift every day this week," one employee reported.

Other employees countered with complaints of moving too slowly. One employee with prior experience in a self-managing system in another industry talked wistfully of the past pleasures of working on a mature self-managing team and of his occasional frustration in this mill because of the seemingly slow progress toward team maturity. Another worker, recognizing the frustrations of others with the slow pace, responded that he was confident that "the whole design would be really great for workers in the long term, but in the short run what was needed was a little more patience."

American cultural perceptions of time frames hold one key to this pacing dilemma. It is undoubtedly difficult for U.S. mill workers to think in terms of time horizons of five years for meeting a long-term goal of mature self-management. This is especially true given the presence of daily and monthly production goals. An example was shared by a team manager who explained how all of his team members had already targeted a particularly high-skilled and prestigious job in a control room as their major career objective. He admired their strong motivation to progress rapidly in their careers but noted ruefully, "They all want to have that job by next year." His concluding remark revealed a curious but very real paradox: "The opportunities for these people are unlimited, but there's a limit to it." (In cultures where employees are accustomed to slower promotions, this self-imposed pressure for job advancement may not represent a serious problem.)

He admired their strong motivation to progress rapidly but noted ruefully, "They all want to have [the best] job by next year."

Another source of pressure for team members arose from the perception that they were temporarily short-handed in some areas of the mill. "We're lean . . . pushed to the limit," complained one employee. He pointed out that corporate resources were available for new equipment and supplies but that top management was reluctant to hire any more workers. Their rationale, which he understood and accepted, was that further hiring now would require that some people be released later (a practice inconsistent with an apparent goal of no layoffs). This was a valid explanation, since he realized that as workers became cross-trained, they would increasingly be able to help out other workers who were experiencing problems on any given day. Thus, in the future, slack human resources would already exist through the cross-training program and could be allocated wherever help was needed.

Ironically, though, working hard and keeping the mill operating well without added personnel actually made it more likely that additional workers would not be hired. (Why should management fix a problem that doesn't really exist?) But to the work system's credit, it was apparent that the mill's long-term success was more important to the workers than their immediate comfort. They conveyed feelings of pride in the mill and their work, and they seemed willing to pay the price for success.

Team Setbacks and Growing Pains

The final phenomenon that team members, managers, and top executives experienced was that initially self-managing teams are fragile, vulnerable entities. Members and leaders realized that they had almost no opportunity to rest on their laurels. One employee stressed that "working in the system is great, but it can be very fragile." He explained that "one moment a team can be really clicking, with things going really well, and the next moment things can be in turmoil, with people hollering at one another and a lot of hard feelings produced."

This reality reflects one element of the organization's mission and philosophy statement, which suggests that "conflict is inevitable," but it must be resolved in a "timely and equitable manner." Team members were learning that disagreements will arise and voices will be raised, but consensus decisions within the teams must be reached and supported for the team to move ahead. Teams will experience both successes and failures, and overall progress will take a lot of work. Without continuous effort, the tremendous investment of time and effort in team development can quickly be destroyed as group members discover that group cohesiveness is a fragile entity.

Conflict is inevitable, but it must be resolved in a timely and equitable manner.

In summary, even in highly successful self-managing team operations, expectations are raised and sometimes not fulfilled, and workers become frustrated. Employees receive a lot of flexibility, responsibility, and variety in their work yet are simultaneously faced with a heavy training load and numerous time-consuming meetings. Team members gradually become able to help one another in significant ways but in the short run may find themselves feeling as if they belong to an understaffed organization. These challenges, combined with the ambiguity and threats that team managers often feel in a new work system, make for some tough times. Add to this the reality that some classes of employees perceive a drop in importance and status as others gain in influence and involvement, and the road to continued progress can seem rocky.

LESSONS FOR FUTURE TEAM OPERATIONS

After one year, self-managing teams at the paper mill were apparently thriving, despite some growing pains and imperfections. Some employees were more enthusiastic than others, but in general, our assessment indicated that the mill's work force was highly committed, involved, and satisfied. Early data for mill efficiency and profitability indicated that they were sharply ahead of even their most optimistic projections.

The decision to emphasize the technical aspects has some clear advantages. Mainly, this approach offers more optimal utilization of the technology in the beginning. Nevertheless, a significant potential disadvantage should be noted. The decision to use a high percentage of managers and experienced workers from other traditional organizations may be an impediment to the social development of self-managing teams. In some ways, Lake Superior has characteristics of a "retrofit" launching of teams rather than a pure "greenfield" launch. It is possible that managers and workers can actually hinder the development of teams because they will not relinquish preestablished attitudes.

The pursuit of business without bosses through self-managing teams is still viewed as a radical work design innovation in most countries and industries, despite fast becoming the norm in new U.S. paper mills. The logic for using teams in this mill seems clear—matching state-of-the-art machinery with a state-of-the-art managerial system.

Perhaps the most challenging question raised by this study is why other firms in other industries have not moved as rapidly toward use of self-managing teams. They can represent a major competitive (yet socially responsible) strategy. Employees at all levels of the mill seemed to be saying, "We couldn't compete, let alone excel, in this industry with a traditional work system that stifles worker contributions." One worker summed up the situation: "I'm amazed that manufacturing hasn't done this earlier. It totally baffles me that America has gone this long without it. Sometimes I wonder how we ever made anything." The insights gained and lessons learned may help other organizations in many countries recognize the value and avoid some of the potential problems in the use of self-managing SuperTeams.

Key Lessons for Creating Business Without Bosses

1. Emphasize the technical side first, before worrying about perfecting the social dimension of the organization. The social side is important but can be viewed in a longer time frame and can be brought along more slowly.
2. Introducing a self-managing team approach into a greenfield site is easier and, all other things being equal, has a better chance for success than trying to change an established system.
3. Real participation, if it pervades the entire organization, will be valued by the majority of employees. There is potentially a high payoff in terms of commitment, satisfaction, and loyalty. However, initial employee desire to participate may differ dramatically.
4. Many employees are hungry to learn and grow as a legitimate route to acquiring power (and money) in organizations. Organizations should feed this appetite by providing opportunities for growth.
5. Employees will experience pressure and stress from the demands of the work system's growing pains (e.g., lots of meetings, a continually changing environment). Support them in their attempts to adjust.
6. Continually support, and seek to clarify, the current and future roles of team managers. Anticipate and monitor their fears, and respond to them.
7. Anticipate that employees (especially those who have the most to lose) will be strongly concerned with equity in their work relationships; consider the impact of actions and decisions on their equity perceptions.
8. Manage team expectations for their own progress by alerting them to the probable long time frames, differential maturation rates across teams, and other potential difficulties.

Chapter 4

The Early
Implementation Phase:
Getting Teams Started in
the Office

This chapter describes the implementation phase that launched self-managing teams in an office environment among knowledge workers. In 1988, after extensive self-analysis, executives of IDS Financial Services decided to undertake a transition to self-managing teams in their mutual funds operations division. Formerly, the organizational and work design of the division could be described as highly differentiated and hierarchical. This story describes the organizational structures that evolved to guide the transition, as well as the most important milestones along the way. The change encountered special problems among the supervisors and senior clerks, who were less than enthusiastic about it. The actual switch was executed over a weekend, using a "big bang" theory of change. Follow-up analysis showed that, despite the problems of transition, a highly effective system resulted. Doing business without bosses created a system that was able to service clients with shorter cycles, higher quality, and more flexibility.

This chapter was written by Henry P. Sims, Jr., Charles C. Manz, and Barry Bateman.

This chapter describes how business without bosses can be applied to an office setting of a company in a service industry. The employees who were the focus of a change to self-managing teams were "knowledge workers"—those whose work is mainly the transformation of information. Relatively little work has been done to apply self-managing teams

85

to an office situation, so the effort we describe here is one of the pioneering changes in the service sector.

The story presented here reviews the early startup stages of self-managing teams in an office situation. The company used the technique of sociotechnical systems (STS) analysis to execute this change. The company pioneering this effort was IDS Financial Services, Inc., of Minneapolis, Minnesota, a subsidiary of American Express Company. The story presents a picture of key structures and processes that are critical for a changeover to a team system. While the story can be described as quite successful, it also provides insight into the challenges, the frustrations, and the difficulties that inevitably accompany such a significant change.

THE ORGANIZATION

IDS, the current name for a company that started as Investors Diversified Services, has been described as the quiet financial giant from Minneapolis. Originally founded in 1894, today it offers a wide range of financial services and products, including personal financial planning, insurance and annuities, mutual funds, certificates, limited partnerships, consumer banking, lending, and brokerage services. The company's products and services are distributed by a nationwide network of more than 6,500 financial planners, whose efforts are supported by more than 3,600 employees in the company's home office.

The change to teams was quite successful, despite the challenges, frustrations, and difficulties.

In 1990, IDS owned or managed more than $58 billion in assets, including $22 billion under management in 36 mutual finds. Since acquired by American Express in 1984, its earnings have grown at a compound annual growth rate of 22 percent.

IDS planners work with individual clients to identify financial goals and objectives and to devise a complete financial strategy tailored to the individual's needs. A client who implements an IDS financial plan typically purchases one or more of the financial products offered by the company. On a day-to-day basis, the financial planners deal with home office service representatives employed by Mutual Fund Operations, now called the Transaction Services Department. Their contact is by mail and telephone and typically involves a transaction on behalf of a client. Thus, the financial planners—independent field agents who interact directly with the client—are highly dependent on the quality, accuracy, and speed of the behind-the-scenes or backroom services provided by employees of the Operations Division.

Nature of the Work at IDS

Fundamentally, IDS's Mutual Fund Operations can be viewed as a service organization that processes information. The prototypical customer is an independent financial planner who has responsibility for providing financial advice to clients. Most of the actual work revolves around an information or financial transaction, typically initiated by mail or telephone—for example, an investment of a certain amount of money in an IDS mutual fund for a client, a withdrawal or redemption from an account, or arranging for a specific payout plan for retirement purposes. The more routine transactions are typically carried out by core workers.

Although most of the transactions are relatively straightforward, some require special technical or legal expertise to ensure compliance with laws and regulations. Transactions that involve interactions with legal trusts or estate settlements require special clerks—individuals with specialized and extensive knowledge who focus on special problems—who are available to support the core workers. Senior clerks served as firefighters, problem solvers, and quasi-supervisors.

Overall, the work can be characterized as an input/output flow of information and financial resources across the organization's boundaries. Although much of the work is impersonal, requiring only action on information flow, a significant element in the process is the interpersonal relationship (by distance) with the financial planners. An important aim of the organization is to retain the planners as satisfied customers. Accuracy and absence of errors are critical for maintaining both efficiency and customer goodwill.

The Competitive Situation

As a part of the change under consideration, the management team in Mutual Fund Operations had assessed the opportunities for improvement that existed within the division and identified the following major business trends:

Major growth in the financial planner and client base.

More home office services being provided directly to clients.

Increasing need for flexibility, especially for changing volumes.

A continuing increase in the number of products sold.

A volatile market.

An increased use of technology by clients, planners, and home office staff.

Increased competition.

Two key questions emerged from this analysis: (1) How can business processing errors be prevented (in essence, the quality issue)? and (2) How can the organization be more adaptable to changing volumes, products, and the financial environment (the flexibility issue)? A partial answer to these questions lies in an expanded utilization of technology, but, most of all, an increased dependence on the quality of the organization's human resources. Issues of quality and flexibility inevitably mean a need for improving the ability and motivation of the organization's work force. One of the alternatives brought forward for consideration was an organizational change to teams.

One key issue is quality. How can processing errors be prevented?

Changing the Work Design

When we collected data for this story, a small portion of the organization had just converted to a self-managing team; the other employees continued to work in the traditional work unit operation. This organizational change was the result of a process of conscious analysis and design that had been sponsored by management and performed by employees who did the work.

Some of the motivation for the change came from a dissatisfaction with the status quo. One manager recognizing this said, "About 30 percent of our staff was assigned to error corrections." Another manager said, "We've done a lot of tweaking in the last few years. The organization is so massive and so complex that we were tweaked out. I think we all realized we needed something new."

The division was profitable, but none of the managers thought that operations were running smoothly. Over the years, the organization had evolved into what one manager described as a patchwork of responsibilities structured by a seemingly illogical combination of function, product, and processes. Job specialization was deeply embedded, and the total organization was described as fragmented. "A customer might call and get transferred four or five times before they could reach someone who could help." Accuracy was a problem. The division had encountered a temporary crisis in 1987 when, during the stock market crash, the system was overloaded and almost collapsed. The average response time to a customer during that day was about seven minutes. Further, the division was generally not regarded as a desirable place to work and had a high turnover rate.

Job specialization was deeply embedded.

Vice-president Bill Scholz brought a special vision to this situation. He foresaw the possibility of the division's sinking to a survivor mode in the future and wanted to act now to preclude this possibility. Over months, he and his staff considered many alternatives, including functional reorganization and supervisory training. After this period of introspection and study, they decided to embark on an organizational redesign effort spearheaded by a sociotechnical systems analysis.

STRUCTURES FOR CHANGE

In order to implement the change, several temporary organizational structures were formed. During the planning stages, the fundamental organizational structure remained intact, but several committees or implementation teams were formed to facilitate the process: the steering committee, the design team, and the pilot team. Each of these teams received process and technical assistance from a consultant team consisting of an inside consultant and an outside consultant experienced in the use of sociotechnical systems analysis.

The Steering Committee

The steering committee was established and convened by Bill Scholz. It consisted of Scholz and his staff of managers (including Jim Punch, then operations manager, now vice-president), the vice-president for management information systems, and the vice-president of human resources, and it was assisted by the small consulting team. One of its members expressed the objectives of the committee in this way: "I think our particular target was getting the program going, the people in place and establishing other guidelines." Another member added, "The objectives never focused on efficiency or on dollar savings. It focused on better accuracy, better service to clients . . . reductions of errors. We didn't say we were going to reduce expenses by a hundred zillion dollars. We have not deviated one iota; we're interested in accuracy; we're interested in quality."

One member commented about the process of the steering committee: "One thing I noticed is the way that we work together on the steering committee. It was very hard because it was very different from how we worked before. Before, it was, 'This is my world and I make the decisions of what happens here.' But it's not what is happening today. This is still a learning process for us."

The steering committee focused on accuracy and better service to clients.

The steering committee preceded the design team and provided initial parameters and periodic guidance to it. One steering committee member provided this viewpoint: "We kept them protected. We got periodic updates of where they were—cut the roadblocks, gained permission. We published parameters or boundaries for them. They also knew we had the right of veto, which was up front. But it's a real change in role from making the decision." Another described the charter to the design committee as "potent"—they were invested with decision-making discretion about anything that was happening in the division. The steering committee empowered the design team.

The steering committee also acted as liaison to top management and other parts of the organization. "We spent a lot of time developing plans to get senior management sold on this thing," and, "We published volumes of questions and answers. We asked ourselves the hardest questions. You're being a pioneer in this deal."

One major issue, job security, was addressed early. "We had a major off-site meeting for all of our employees when the thing kicked off. We took them to a hotel and gave them croissants and walked them through it. We guaranteed employment for everybody right off the bat. No loss of employment will occur because of the process. We didn't say your job won't change."

The steering committee had to be sensitive to the degree to which they provided guidance to the design team. Bill Scholz "gave them as much freedom as possible, because I didn't want anything to impact the decision. I even told the design team that I'd not be seen."

One senior manager talked about his mixed reactions to the process: "I found the process somewhat painful. Being senior in years and having enjoyed traditional organizations all my career, and now coming to the end of my career—But, it's really been refreshing. It put some new excitement into the last few years." Several managers wondered whether employees would be able to make decisions of the same quality as managers. Despite these reservations, the steering committee decided to proceed and announced the prospective change to the entire division. The next step was the formation of the design team.

The Design Team

The design team was selected from 57 volunteers. One member explained, "Everybody was invited to a meeting that explained the process. I listened to what they were proposing, and I did apply for a position on the team." Another said, "We were afraid it was an efficiency drive. In fact, it wasn't. It was right up front that there would be no jobs lost because of this project."

The steering committee empowered the design team.

The design team was composed of 11 people—8 core workers, 2 supervisors, and 1 senior clerk—and was supported by the professional external consultant who was experienced with STS analysis. No formal leader was designated.

Each team member was relieved of his or her usual job and devoted full time to the design team efforts, meeting every day from 8:00 A.M. to 4:30 P.M., and meeting with the steering committee about once every two weeks to exchange information and seek guidance. The original plan called for the design team to accomplish its objectives in three to six months. In fact, the team's efforts took eight and a half months.

The team followed three major steps: developing a plan, conducting the technical (task) analysis, and doing the social analysis. Data gathering and analysis included interviewing and surveying the financial planners, clients, and employees; documenting work flows; and identifying errors and determining causes of key variance.

Team members described the communication climate with the steering committee as "mediocre to fair." One team member characterized it as "very, very difficult. It's probably the major problem in the process. We were supposed to do things by consensus decision. And it's a terrible, tedious, long process with all those people. And everybody had to have a role in making their viewpoint known. It takes a long time to learn how to do that without wasting time."

One or two members came close to leaving the team. "Burnout—communication problems," one said. "I felt like I was going to go crazy. The team had high expectations that we could sit in the meeting and, in half an hour, go right through issues and get the decisions made. The design team was highly motivated, and expectations of what they could achieve were very high. Perhaps we were too perfectionist."

The role of the supervisor received considerable attention from the design team. "The existing supervisors were given a lot of attention. They were quite nervous about the whole process. One of the rumors they'd heard about STS is that supervisors were to be eliminated." In fact, supervisors were not eliminated, although their role was changed considerably. Their title was changed to "facilitator," and "their goal would be to enable the team to become self-directing." One design team member anticipated problems with both supervisors and managers: "They will have difficulty adapting. The problem of this process is that the managerial staff have difficulty letting go of decision making. They will need to learn how to allow the team to make decisions."

The design team determined that teams would be organized according to geographical or regional lines and that each team would have 25 to 40 members. When questioned whether this number might be too large, one design team member replied, "We actually have teams within the teams." Each team was intended to be multifunctional; it would include all of the different functions and processes within the organization, and it would be empowered to make the decisions needed to process the work in a timely and accurate fashion.[1]

The steering committee focused on accuracy and better service to clients.

Most of all, the design team emphasized how the work could be designed to improve effectiveness. One member said, "Effectiveness really highlights what we wanted to get at, and that was quality. We wanted to do the work right the first time and to eliminate the errors out there. We wanted the work to be done effectively so that we don't have to go back and do it again." This analysis was undertaken via the sociotechnical system process, a formal approach to analyzing the technical part of the work and the social interaction part of it. (See box.)

What Is STS?

Sociotechnical design, also known as STS (sociotechnical systems), a systematic approach to the design of work, involves a thorough analysis of both the technical (the tools and techniques used in the production or information flow process) and social (how work is divided and coordinated) components of a work system.

Typically organizations tend to place more priority on one aspect at the expense of the other. STS seeks to avoid this imbalance, assuming that both aspects are equally important in controlling error (variance from standards). Controlling key variances is seen as the central challenge in producing a quality product or service at the lowest possible cost.

The approach, which differs from more traditional industrial engineering design, views meeting employee needs for personal control and autonomy as critical in controlling variance. According to STS, the best way for variance to be controlled is for the employee who performs the task to be aware of the variance and to make the necessary correction.

An in-depth analysis of the work system provides a complete picture of the environment, work flow, communication flow, technical problems, and other issues inherent in any modern work organization. When the analysis is done by people who do the actual work, their knowledge base increases substantially. Closer to the core work, they are able to use the knowledge to solve problems more effectively.

The following diagram provides an overall picture of the major components of an STS design effort. It consists of three primary steps: an environmental scan, a technical analysis, and a social analysis.

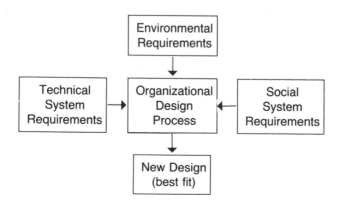

The environmental scan, done first, includes reviewing the history, culture, goals, structure, and economic and marketing context of the organization. Inputs, outputs, and overall technology are also considered. The technical analysis, done next, breaks down the work flow into tasks, which are grouped into unit operations. Variances are tracked and recorded on a key variance control chart, and variances that a group inherits from the outside are separated from those that are produced internally.

Once key variances are understood, an analysis of the social system is conducted to see how those variances are being controlled. The social system review also addresses communication patterns and other organization climate issues. Finally, these analyses are all integrated into a new design recommendation.

This analysis is a demanding and challenging undertaking. Sufficient time must be allowed to accomplish it.

How did management react to the fact that the design team took 8½ rather than 3 months? One of the steering committee members reflected, "By the time we got into the technical analysis, it was clear that we weren't going to get done in 3½ months. We really muddled through the technical analysis. That was probably the most frustrating phase. (But), we had to stick with it and go with it, because we didn't have any option."

One factor that caused a substantial roadblock was the issue of how the redesign efforts should deal with the existing system of measuring work output. A considerable amount of money had been invested in this system. According to one source, "This measurement system was designed by traditional industrial engineers according to classic industrial engineering principles." That is, the intent was to increase efficiency and enforce standards by implementing a high degree of control over the employees. The system, described by one organization member as an "automated tracking system" and by another as a "computerized electronic surveillance system," was a sophisticated automatic logging and data tracking system that measured each employee's work behavior to a remarkable degree. Certainly individual employees were evaluated according to the numbers they produced.

The system had negative side effects. According to one member of the organization, "A core worker would not leave her post in order to solve a problem because it would affect her performance numbers. Customers would suffer because they would not solve the customer's problem." Job satisfaction was low and turnover was high.

The design committee initially wanted to scrap the system, but others pointed out the importance of the statistics that were derived from it, especially the notion that these statistics were necessary as feedback if the teams were to manage themselves. Eventually the committee recommended that a modified form of the system be retained; most important, the main use of the system output would be for teams to manage their own system.

Another sticky issue revolved around the role of the quality assurance group, currently an external structure that functioned mainly for control purposes. The eventual recommendation was that most of these quality assurance personnel would be brought into the service teams.

What should be done with the current quality assurance group?

Another factor that affected the amount of time the design team spent was the question of how much it should set minimum critical specifications and how much detail should be left to the teams. In retrospect, one member felt the design team design was overspecified:[2] "In hindsight, we have concluded that they spent too much time and effort and intensity of overstructuring, too much detail in terms of task. I think the teams could figure it out. Where do you draw the line between what the design team recommends versus the discretion that you give the team?" Another manager demurred, "But I think the level of detail was needed for the design team to have a deep understanding before they went ahead and tried to figure out a structure. Even though it wasn't used in a final design, all of that detail—they needed that."

Another post hoc issue is whether the design team should have been assigned full time to the design process. One manager said, "I think the major mistake we made as a steering group is that we allowed this to be a full-time job for the design team. I'll tell you, you sit in a room every day, no matter how well you like somebody, five days in a row, three months straight, and you're into this analysis poop, I think you start questioning the meaning of life."

Another problem developed: a "we" versus "they" phenomenon between members of the design team and other members of the work force. One design team member broached this issue: "There was some reaction to the design team . . . privileged and elitist. You were chosen; we were not."

Despite the difficulties, in the end, one manager commented about the design team, "(It) was a breakthrough for us . . . they became really empowered. They had a lot of power, and they knew it." The design team did indeed accomplish its objectives and produced a complete set of recommendations that seemed to be generally acceptable to various constituencies:[3]

1. Teams should be formed around customers/planners clustered within a geographical region.

2. Team members should be trained to perform multiple skills and tasks. That is, each team should have the ability to service virtually all requests made by clients and their planners.

Teams were formed around a geographical region. Teams are multifunctional.

---

3. Team size should be about 30 to 40 employees—large enough to handle regional volume and provide technical expertise yet small enough to provide free-flowing communication and a sense of belonging. The notion of multiple skills was an important point of the recommendation. That is, a team will possess the skills and knowledge required to accomplish a wide range of tasks. It will have the capability to process transactions from start to finish.

4. The role of supervisor was to change to that of a team facilitator who would work with the team to establish goals and objectives, provide liaison with other teams and outside groups, project team volumes and staffing needs, participate in performance discussions, manage projects, and facilitate team building and conflict resolution.

5. An important recommendation was the reconceptualization of the role of the managers in the division. The previous role of managers had been described as "fire fighters" and "watchers

who watch the watchers"! Managers were described as "focusing their energy downward and inward—not out to the environment, nor forward into the future."

The role of managers would change to strategic director, with primary responsibility for managing the interface with the outside world, dealing with long-term strategic issues, helping to create new systems, coaching team leaders, and coordinating across the organization.[4] At the time data were collected for this story, the changeover to the strategic director role had not been implemented. However, the current manager team had accepted the recommendation of the change in management role. (An interesting aspect of this recommendation is that the role of these managers had essentially been redesigned by the *subordinates* of the managers, and the managers had accepted this redesign.)

6. Information systems would be developed that would provide each team with the information it needs to operate efficiently as a small business. These included measures of quality and quantity of transactions.

The design team's timetable for change started with a single pilot team, formed around a specific geographical area. Later, the remainder of the employees would be formed into teams at a single time, popularly referred to as the "big bang," that also corresponded with a move of the physical premises.

The Pilot Team

At the time of data collection, the pilot team had been in existence for only a month, yet the enthusiasm of the members was obvious. "I've been on the team for about a month. I've made some significant contributions," said one member. The team consisted of about 25 employees (some from the design team) with two facilitators.

From management's point of view, an effective training program had been undertaken prior to the pilot team start-up, yet the employees did not see it this way. One month into start-up, one of the facilitators said: "The training needs have not been met. The people feel frustrated because they've been a file clerk or they've been a filmer, and they want to learn to be a phone rep or a letter correspondent or whatever, and they haven't had the opportunity to train. It all takes time." Also, it soon became obvious that a skills development opportunity was necessary. The team first conducted a skills analysis to identify what would be needed to carry out the expanded responsibilities. Next, an analysis was done, and a team facilitator helped to create and balance the skills among team members.

Clearly the pilot team was in a mood for learning and experimentation. One member said, "If we were in an old unit, they might have said [about a suggestion for change], 'Well, we can't do it. It's not feasible. Forget it.' Now, they bring the idea to the team, and the team says, 'Oh yes. We think this will work.' It's a chance to try ideas, and if they fall on their face, then that's the opportunity they had to do it. We're not going to say we're closing the door. You feel more important. You do what you can."

On the team, there's a chance to try ideas.

The feeling of control and authority was apparent: "I feel like I'm making more supervisory decisions than I've ever been allowed to before—as far as transactions are concerned. I can present myself as the authority in what I do, because I am." Another member said, "My definition of fun is: interesting. Also, being able to make a difference in what's going on, as opposed to sitting back and observing things."

The factor of teamwork came through loud and clear when pilot team members talked about their work. "When you're working in a very, very small group, you are accountable for how many calls you take and the quality that you put into your work, the amount of effort . . . you're going to find it's going to come back to you." One employee said: "We don't go to the facilitator and say, 'Can I have the day off?' and expect them to find somebody to cover for us. We check it out with the people in our group."

Learning to work together as a team is not always smooth or without some difficulties. "Right now on the pilot team, we're experiencing some frustrations, some blockage points. There are some issues that we have to address—about how to make decisions or who has the responsibility to make decisions in certain areas." Differences in styles become apparent: "I like to get everything done quickly and get it out of the way. And some people need more time to deliberate. We're working through a lot of style issues. As a result, you're not going to see 100 percent of us happy." Overall, however, even at this early stage, the pilot team seemed to be experiencing some successes.

WHAT REALLY HAPPENED: BUMPS ALONG THE WAY

Several issues seemed to be apparent during our visit. Among the problems were negative anticipation, the transition from supervisor to facilitator, anxiety from supervisors not yet on teams, and perceived decline in the status of senior clerks.

Negative Anticipation

Not all employees were looking forward to the team system. One employee described some co-workers as not wanting to change: "They don't want to have to learn these things. They say, 'I hope they fall on their face because then we don't have to do that.'" Another said, "I hear a lot of negative feedback. Some people say, 'I don't even want to try it.' Either you are strongly for it or you are strongly against it." Indeed, there were very few in the middle: "Either you were strongly for it or you were strongly against it. It was either one or the other."

Some didn't want to try the team system.

But, it appears that much of this negative attitude is subject to change once the team system is actually experienced. One team member describes her initial reaction: "I hated the idea. I just despised it. I wanted to back out. I told my supervisor, 'I don't want anything to do with it.' Now that I'm active in it (the team), and participate more, I feel 'isn't this great?'"

The Transition from Supervisors to Facilitators

Two facilitators, both supervisors before the introduction of teams, were assigned to the pilot team. They found the team environment to be substantially different. Noted one of them, "We're finding that making decisions with 25 to 30 people is something that's completely different. Just getting to decide how the decisions are going to be made can be overwhelming as we experience it." She elaborated on this difference:

> "In the traditional system it was clear that I had the final word, and right now it is not clear. That's different. Another thing that's different is that we have changed the tasks. It's one thing to be self-managing in your old room and doing the same function, but now we've put together 20 other types of jobs that we didn't know anything about, so instead of having one set of goals and objectives, we've got a variety of them.
>
> "For example, I previously supervised a unit that processed new business. Now, the team has new business, redemptions, change of ownership, service—many different things—all of the functions that now revolve around a geographical area."

The other facilitator agreed, commenting on the need to become knowledgeable in a considerably enlarged area of service: "It becomes frustrating because you felt like you should be knowing it, but you don't, and yet we know that it's unrealistic for us to think at this point that we can know everything. We make it a learning experience, and it takes a lot of time to do that."

Facilitators try to instill confidence in the new team members as they undertake new responsibilities: "One woman expressed a need just to run exceptions by one of us. She probably has more knowledge than we do, but she also was not one that handled the exceptions in her former unit. When something comes up, she said, 'It would be nice if you were here so I can run it by you.' She's feeling that it's not traditional for her to do this and psychologically is not confident that what she decides would be accepted. She might be looking for a little bit of a security blanket."

Another example was cited: "Initially when she came and asked me the question, I said, 'What would you do if nobody else was available?' It's asking them to become independent. You have to spend the time with people to get them to that comfort level and to build up their self-confidence."

The system surrounding the team must change too. One facilitator said, "Some of the frustrations we have are really related to the transition . . . fumbling around with getting reports started up, system authorizations, and a lot of technical information because we've never done anything like this before. We're spending so much time on these start-up issues." Like right now, for instance, we don't even have some measures. We're just in the process of getting quality measure for some of the people.

It's asking them to become independent.

Clearly, teams can learn through their mistakes, and the facilitator realized this, even to the point of allowing mistakes to happen occasionally. "Their first opportunity to display self-management was when they made the decision to have a person gone [leaving a station unmanned] when someone left the room. It was a small, minor thing, but it was a simple lesson. They made the wrong decision, and through that decision we learned, and we discussed it as a learning tool. We talked about the work flow and responsibility to cover their work and stuff. It was a valuable experience."

One of the pilot team members discussed the change in the supervisor's role: "There's an incredible redesigning of some of the power that goes with supervising people. Letting go of some of the responsibility and letting go of some of the control that you had previously is a serious deal, and I'm sure it's very threatening." "We don't really think of our facilitators as being supervisors. It's not 'you can do this no you can't.' They help us."

The motivation to be a facilitator is complex and not always immediately evident:

"The thing I've been struggling with is that there's nothing to call my own. Eventually, if they're truly self-managing, it's going to be the team that gets most of the recognition. And that part is going to be hard, because I think traditionally the recognition that the unit's doing good would start with the supervisor, and you'd feel like, 'I really did something here on my own, an accomplishment.' But now I get more satisfaction out of helping someone to do something rather than telling them to do it."

The second facilitator agreed with this perspective:

"I think basically we're all human, and where I would be very glad to have the team take the credit, nevertheless, my humanness says to me, 'I really would enjoy it if just occasionally somebody would pat *me* on the back and say, "Hey, you're doing a good job today." ' Sometimes you wonder if people you're working with realize the touchy position that the facilitator is put in because you have a strategic director up here expecting big things from you, and you have a whole team expecting their needs from you, and we're kind of like a pickle in the middle of a sandwich, and we don't know which side of the bread we should be on. Does the word 'facilitator' really give credit where credit is due?"

"I get more satisfaction out of helping than telling."

The traditional conflict of the supervisor as the person in the middle is still there with the facilitator role: "Right now, my strategic director is expecting some reports, and I'm finding some difficulty getting him the data that he needs, and, at the same time, the team has needs, and I'm feeling like I'm sitting in the middle here, and it's not a very good feeling."

In this early stage of the team development, the issue of goals and objectives was not yet resolved:

"In a traditional structure of supervision, you'd have goals and objectives; it was laid out. I always felt I knew what part of the path I was traveling on. Here as a team facilitator, so far I haven't felt that clarified yet, so I don't quite know where we're going. Part of the problem is the strategic directors, the persons we directly report to. After all this length of time, I think the strategic directors still do not have a real clear picture of how they fit into this, and this is kind of confusing to me.

"Before, it was the supervisor reporting to your manager, and your manager reporting to your vice-president and so on. Now, I kind of feel like there are several people out there giving input to what I should be doing and one day it may be coming from one person directly, but indirectly I sometimes feel like it's coming from several."

Another put it this way: "They listen to what we say and they can put in their input if they disagree, but if the majority of the team says 'it's gonna work,' then, we'll try it."

At one month into the pilot team start-up, the facilitators were probably at a point of maximum ambiguity and frustration. "The reorganization of the task and the structure of the task are one dimension, and the management style or the division of authority, if you will, is a different dimension." The facilitators seemed to be faced with a double-barreled change.

Finally, since the major changeover had not yet occurred, the change in the role of the managers to strategic directors had not yet taken place. We suspected that the managers, like the supervisors, would also be likely to experience some ambiguity, tension, and anxiety as their role changed over the next few months.

Supervisor Anxiety

Supervisors not yet on teams were anxious. "One of the first things I remember was, 'Oh, we're going to go on this team-based kind of operation and everybody's going to have to know everything.' I think that tended to spook people." Another question loomed large: "Will I lose my job as a supervisor? If the role of supervisor is going to change, does that mean some of us will be out of a job?"

Management made substantial efforts to counter the fear of loss of job security. One supervisor said, "They had several meetings to alleviate those fears and assured everyone that they would not lose their job.

Their role would change in many respects. People might be doing something else, but everybody's going to do something."

But some supervisors eagerly looked forward to "big bang" day, when all of the other departments would be changed over to the team system. One supervisor said, "I'm delighted. I think that it's going to make jobs a lot more interesting for people. I think there will be a lot more buy-in to decisions if it's a group decision than if it's mine." Another also expressed confidence and optimism: "Almost every week that passes, something tends to be cleared up. As we get closer and closer, 'Ah hah! So that's how it's going to be. That's great.' Weekly, we just feel more and more comfortable with it." Part of this optimism came from observations of the pilot team. One supervisor noted that "the pilot team is working. They're getting work done. Nobody's quit. They're not beating each other up. Things are going fine. The people that I've talked to who are on the pilot team said very positive things. Plus, we've been given a massive amount of training."

Finally, an interesting phenomenon seemed to be taking place: All of the attention surrounding the change seemed to be having an influence on the supervisors. Some supervisors were beginning to change their behavior even before being assigned to teams.

The Senior Clerks

Perhaps one group more than any other saw themselves as losers in this change to teams—the senior clerks. A senior clerk is a special problem solver—an hourly employee who has special knowledge and authority and a higher rate of pay. One senior clerk described the job in this way: "I investigate, I dig, I work on problem cases, I work with the supervisor on administrative things and attend different meetings, and I enjoy what I'm doing now."

In the new system, the position of senior clerk would not exist. All employees would be team members, and each team member would be expected to perform a fair amount of the work. As one supervisor put it: "Well, this is part of the senior clerk's problem. Right now, most senior clerks do not process. They don't write letters, they don't answer the phone, they don't process applications—only problems. So some of them have expressed distress that they're going to have to go back to processing than more of a consultant/training/question-answer problem solver. I'm not sure that's going to be resolved." Another supervisor said: "Now, they have a certain amount of prestige—they get more money. Everybody else can move up and learn a bunch of other things. The senior clerks are already up there."

One senior clerk directly addressed the issue in this way: "I'm going to be doing core work again, and I feel like it's a step backward. I took the training to be a senior clerk. And just as you learn and work toward certain goals and when you reach those goals, then you find out you're put into a team, and the goals and the titles you have achieved, they're no longer there. You're just like anyone else. It will be harder in a team." Uncertainty and anxiety among the senior clerks were high: "A lot of this stuff is still up in the air. If you are a senior clerk, you're losing out on that prior learning process. There's a lot of unknowns out there, and they can't really tell you because they don't know."

Uncertainty among senior clerks seemed to be at a maximum.

Senior clerks expressed skepticism about the team's ability to do error-free work: "Who's going to catch a mistake? It's really scary because there are so many different procedures involved in dealing with attorneys, documents. There's so many things to remember. I fear there may be more errors because I don't know who's going to be catching them." And another expressed doubt over the competence of ordinary employees: "They skim over things; they don't double-check everything. So the error rate goes up. They don't want to learn anything. Some of them are worried about going into the team because they just want to do the job they are doing. They need to get input from us." Further, "When you learn the job, it's a lot to learn. There's a lot to look for, a lot to check for. And there's sometimes a person that just can't cut it. Who's going to know?"

PRELIMINARY RESULTS

Since the pilot team had been underway for only a month at the time of our interviews, quantitative information about their performance was not yet available. Yet some changes were clearly taking place in several areas:

- Confidence for improvement: "We feel that we'll be able to increase our average speed of answer, and our 'abandon rate' (unanswered calls) will decrease proportionally."

- The idea of team ownership: "You feel that what you are doing is actually making money for your team. We are our own little company. Every time we loan ourselves out to somebody, we know we're going to charge that other unit $35 an hour. It makes you feel better."

- The issue of quality: "You work more thoroughly. You want to make sure that you don't let the errors leave the unit. You also see where all the work goes. You feel more complete if you know the work is going to be done."

You don't let the errors leave the unit.

- Flexibility of operations: "One thing that I see as a really great benefit, even in the short term, is that we are able to be more flexible and respond to volumes quicker than previous. Our volumes fluctuate very heavily because of client whims and market fluctuations. I was spending a lot of time sitting, waiting for something to do. Now, we've arranged something where I can get work from other areas and help them while I'm waiting to serve my clients." Another supported this idea: "There's a high degree of flexibility that I don't think there was before. There are some jobs, such as mine, that it's critical that I be there when the phones open, because that's a client service element. I promised the client that I'd be there at 7 A.M., and I have to; I don't have a choice."

One result of the team implementation is that pilot team members were beginning to develop a more personal relationship with the financial planners in the field. Their contact with these planners is strictly through the mail or over the telephone:

"I've never met them. I do speak to clients and planners on a daily basis. Now, since I have my own area, I speak to the same people many times a week. Now the planner knows you by name. Even though you've never met a person, you establish a rapport with somebody over a period of time because of repetition, rather than one of 10,000 or whatever. You can deal on a one-to-one relationship and establish that, yes, despite the fact that our planners are independent businessmen, they are also part of our team. We have already received a couple of letters, and it makes you feel, 'Gee, I am really doing something for the people out there.' And, they do appreciate what we are doing."

Sometimes pilot team members have taken on the role of informal trainer to field financial planners:

"I find it easier to educate the planners when they trust you. There are some things that all planners don't necessarily know that would make it easier for them and their clients to do business. I don't say, 'Hey, you're doing this wrong.' That's not my idea of feedback. But if somebody is consistently doing things that are incorrect, just some feedback on that issue can prevent a lot of miscommunication or errors from happening. If I see the same planner do the same thing, you talk to them all the time, you feel like, 'I think it'd be easier if you kinda went like this, or, you did that.' I would help them. Now they say, 'I know I can call somebody, and not just call a number and never know who you're going to get. I can personally ask for this person, and I can get this person. I know who you are. You've helped me.' It makes me think, 'Hey, maybe I *can* make a difference.' "

This attitude extends to the clients: "We've also suggested that we would like the clients' response also, not just the planners. We'd like the clients to say, 'Am I getting a better result now that we can call direct?' "

I *can* make a difference!

In the pilot team, the error rate was already beginning to decline, and the team members were very much aware of the output measure.

"We had like 70 percent accuracy before. Now, it's always at least 99 to 100 percent every day. Now, we see that one day of the week we'll have one error, out of five days." Another team member said, "Yesterday it was 100 percent accuracy, and we were happy because nothing was out of our hands, and we felt really good because all these transactions went out error free."

With the team concept, the feedback loop to the team member was much more complete: "We used to have specialists. If you had an error on an application, you couldn't do anything with it, and we send it to a specialist. From there on we'd never see the application again. But now, you hold it. You call the planner. It comes right back to you, so you see it. You started it, and now it's finished. We feel more of a completion. We don't feel like it's half done and it's still floating and you don't know."

CONCLUSIONS

Conversion of an existing organization to a team system is indeed a rocky road in the beginning. Many employees and managers are at a peak of frustration because of the uncertainty of how to get ready or how to react to the change. Yet the conversion to a team system yields obvious rewards. First, most workers seem to gain in status and perceptions of power. Despite initial difficulties in seeing benefits, managers also gain through greater productivity, better quality, and generally reduced tension and conflict at work. Thus, both managers and workers can benefit significantly and experience an increase in their own ability to influence the system and performance.

Many challenges emerge as well, and none is more central than the issue of the changing role of supervisors and middle managers. Ambiguity and the threat of loss of status and control can make the transition difficult. The most important factor is to recognize the issue as a potential critical difficulty and to take steps to deal with it.

Supervisors frequently see themselves as losing in power and prestige. The issue seems to be especially salient when an existing system, with existing supervisors, is changed to a team system. Frequently the supervisors are converted from a traditional system of authority to a system where they are called facilitators, coaches, or coordinators. One supervisor expressed his contempt for the term "facilitator" by calling it "wimpy." These supervisors-turned-facilitators see themselves as having the same responsibility as before, and maybe more, but they no longer have the same power. Nor do they know how to behave in order to adapt and thrive under a team system.

Training is necessary if current supervisors are to be converted to facilitators, but it is not the complete answer. One strategy that seems to help is to have new facilitators do site visits with veteran facilitators who are experienced and successful at working with a team system. The new facilitator learns more from observing a successful model than any training can provide.

Finally, our own observation is that many people can succeed in this transition to facilitator, but not everyone is capable of completing this emotional philosophical journey. In the end, some supervisors must be replaced because they are incapable of abandoning their previously learned behaviors. It is important to undertake this replacement in a humane, sensitive way. For example, some supervisors can be converted to technical specialists.

Team members are faced with major adjustments and challenges as well. One of the clear messages of the team approach is that employees are expected to use their head as well as their hands. They have a responsibility to try to make their job easier and better.

In any change to a team system, some people see themselves as winning; others see themselves as losing. Often the power base is knowledge. Knowledge has power. Sometimes existing knowledge is invested in the supervisors or in technical specialists, such as the senior clerks at IDS. People who currently have knowledge—the knowledge elite—may be reluctant to share it or facilitate making knowledge more widely diffused. Yet increasing the knowledge of the ordinary employee lies at the core of the team concept. Widespread knowledge is necessary for team success.

Some people see themselves as winning, some as losing.

Despite the significant challenges in converting, team efforts are worthwhile doing. Employees are both excited and exciting. If you listen to their own words, you understand why a conversion to a team system can be a very constructive step. Despite being at a point of maximum uncertainty, the people at IDS were charged up about teams. They valued the strengthening of their linkage to the clients and realized that they could serve clients better. Most of all, they liked the fun of teams, and they realized that at last they could have an impact. As one pilot team member put it, "I really like the idea of being able to make a difference in what's going on, as opposed to sitting back."

Will the same desire for competitiveness drive service systems in the way that manufacturing systems have been driven in recent years? We expect so. The *Wall Street Journal* gave somewhat of an advance indication of this trend with one article recently: "American Firms Send Office Work Abroad To Use Cheap Labor."[5] We believe that work team systems, like the one at IDS, hold tremendous promise for improving competitiveness (as well as quality of work life for employees) in the service sector. Service firms can conduct business without bosses.

POSTSCRIPT: HOW DID THE CHANGE ACTUALLY WORK OUT?

How did all of this actually work out? Did the big bang actually take place? Was it a success? Does IDS still have teams? Since the original information for this chapter was collected in mid-1989, we had the opportunity to seek later information from IDS. Following is a brief update as of early 1992.

The Big Bang

Over a single weekend, IDS converted to a team organization. This "big bang" was undertaken in conjunction with a physical move to new premises.

Many of the quality indicators immediately shot up.

Many expected a short-term decrease in quality and productivity immediately after the move. Others echoed the old refrain: "This is just

111

not going to work." In fact, the opposite happened. Many of the quality indicators immediately shot up. Backlogs seemed to disappear. It was almost as if the teams were determined to show that this new organization was better from the very beginning.

Handling the Mini-Crash Crisis

One of the more interesting indicators was the difference between the way the organization handled a mini-crash, in 1989 (after teams) versus the mini-crash of 1987 (before teams). Of course, a mini-crash is a precipitous falloff in the prices in stocks, mainly on the New York Stock Exchange. A mini-crash influences mutual fund operations by generating an extremely large surge in customer telephone calls—mainly requests for redemptions (customers want to withdraw funds before the market falls further). From an operations viewpoint, the traffic of incoming calls is increased suddenly and immensely, and the challenge to the organization is to respond to this surge.

During the 1987 market crash, the call volume to the organization quadrupled within one day, placing a tremendous load on the transaction system. The result, according to one individual, was chaos. Another called the day a disaster. (Remember that this gloomy event occurred under the old traditional/functional organizational system.)

In October 1989, subsequent to the change to the team system, there was another stock market crash of similar proportions. This crash occurred on a Monday, but movements in the market had presented some indications of impending trouble the previous Friday. On this particular Friday, the entire management group (now called strategy directors) was absent from the office, attending an off-site strategic planning meeting. Thus, they were not present to help plan for the anticipated surge in transactions.

One manager, who returned to the office about 5:00 P.M. on Friday, became aware of the potential situation for the following Monday. He also found that the teams had anticipated the possibility of a surge. Each, on its own, had implemented a plan of how to deal with a surge. For example, most of the teams had decided that several members should report early, they had arranged to work through their lunches, and they had made arrangements with other parts of the IDS organization for backup people to be immediately available to answer the telephones. When Monday came and the mini-crash did occur, people at IDS were very active and working hard, but it almost seemed like a nonevent—no panic, no hysteria, no confusion.

"This team concept really works!"

The following day, when the volume numbers were available, many were surprised to discover that IDS actually took more calls on Monday than in the 1987 crash. For many, it didn't seem possible. Perhaps the strongest indicator of their strength was the average speed of answer—that is, how long it takes to begin to service a call. In 1987, the average speed was 7½ minutes (an indicator of information gridlock). In 1989, the average was *13 seconds!*

This comparison deserves a second look:

1987, before teams	7½ minutes
1989, after teams	13 seconds

One manager said, "This team concept really works!" We might say it a different way. Remember the absence of managers on the critical Friday, when the planning to handle the surge of redemptions was carried out by the teams themselves. This event was a classic example of doing business without bosses. Today, the team system at IDS is alive and well. Most of all, the experience at IDS is one of the early examples that teams are not only appropriate for manufacturing environments, but will work with information workers as well.

Key Lessons for Creating Business Without Bosses

1. Implementing teams requires putting into place well-thought-out structures for guiding and designing the change/implementation effort; for example, a steering committee, a design team, and so on.

2. Sociotechnical systems (STS) analysis and design principles can be used to help guide the implementation. An STS approach offers important benefits but entails significant costs and is quite time-consuming.

3. Special attention should be devoted to equipping supervisors and managers to make the transition successfully to the new role of leading self-managing teams. (See Chapter 2 for more detail.)

4. Implementation of teams typically results in winners and losers. Careful consideration must be given to how teams can be a winning proposition for as many as possible.

5. The road to implementing teams is long and difficult. Have realistic expectations about the amount of time and energy required and patience in waiting for results.

6. Teams are not just for manufacturing systems. Introducing teams in offices in service organizations holds much promise.

Chapter **5**

The Illusion of Self-Management: Using Teams to Disempower

Can self-managing teams be introduced without a top management commitment to doing business without bosses? This chapter tells the story of an independent insurance company in which service teams were introduced to disempower employees and to increase management control. The CEO saw the potential for teams to provide peer pressure and points of leverage for increasing his control of employees. That an illusion of self-management can be created raises a sobering caution. Teams can potentially be used to increase boss control from the top, thus contradicting the philosophy of business without bosses and destroying the potential for empowered superteams.

This chapter was written by Charles C. Manz and Harold L. Angle.

Self-management and self-managing teams have usually been regarded as the opposite of "boss" control; they are associated with doing business without bosses. This view of self-management, however, has been challenged. Some authors, for example, have suggested that close external supervision is not always inconsistent with self-management.[1] When requirements of a job and the information needed to do it are unclear, some management that defines the job's limits can aid a self-managed employee. In fact, defining the limits of employee discretion can be the primary management task. Nevertheless, these limits can significantly constrain and control self-managed employees. As a result, apparent self-management can sometimes be more of an illusion than a reality.

Such challenges to the conventional view of self-management can enrich our understanding of various degrees of employee self-influence. Perhaps it is unrealistic ever to view self-management as a complete absence of external control. On the contrary, people, behavior, and the external environment influence one another.[2] Furthermore, self-management behavior itself requires some support and reinforcement; it can be very difficult for employees to self-manage without encouragement and incentives from the organization.

Perhaps it is unrealistic ever to view self-management as a complete absence of external control.

The important point is that self-management does not operate in a vacuum. Many external factors foster or constrain the process. One important set of external influences involves the dynamics of work groups within which self-managed employees often find themselves.

This chapter describes an independent insurance firm, specializing in industrial casualty loss coverage, that had recently introduced self-managing work teams. This story is especially interesting because the teams were introduced in an industry that historically has tended to emphasize individual self-management. In this case, however, introducing teams actually placed limits on individual freedom and control. The chapter addresses the question, "In an industry having a deeply ingrained cultural norm of individualism, can team self-management come to represent a loss of personal control?"

THE COMPANY AND THE TEAM SYSTEM

The organization is an independent property and casualty insurance firm that employed 32 people at the time we studied it. The firm was founded in 1941—a time when the independent operation, consisting of one or two agents supported by one or two secretaries, was the industry standard. Typically, even when multiagent organizations were established, these tended to be loose associations of loners, each having a network of highly personal relationships with clients. As a rule, there was little need for coordination, and each account executive operated within a set of rules and procedures, as a relatively independent agent.

In the mid-1970s, changes in the legislative environment led to strong competitive pressures in the insurance industry. Efficiency (e.g., in developing client insurance programs, in collection policies) and synergy (optimizing combined efforts) in the efforts of different persons within an agency became very important. Many of the single-agent establishments were either forced out of business or forced to merge into multiagent organizations. Despite the economic pressures that made such changes necessary, this move was frequently a difficult transition for agents accustomed to autonomy.

Less than a year before we began our research, a recently hired vice-president and chief operating officer became acting chief executive officer (CEO). One of his initial acts was to restructure the firm into a set of self-managing work teams. The team philosophy was explained to the employees when the system was introduced, and teams were encouraged to make decisions and solve their problems jointly.

The work system appeared similar to designs used in self-managing team applications in other industries. Within established company guidelines, work teams were expected to be self-managing units that carried out the activities needed for acquiring and servicing accounts cooperatively. The intent of the CEO appeared to be to pass on what were formerly management responsibilities to the teams, with the intended result of more efficient work performance. At the same time, it was apparent that the CEO felt that the company needed to increase its organization and coordination of work efforts. He hoped that the teams would help him achieve efficiencies that would boost the firm's profitability. Thus, although the teams were similar in appearance to self-managing teams found in other work settings (in which team members coordinate their efforts on tasks and work together to solve team problems and make joint decisions), they were apparently implemented with the objective of increasing organizational control from the top—to increase the influence of bosses.

Self-managed teams were implemented with an actual objective of facilitating organizational control.

Under the new system, three teams were created. The senior team consisted of the senior, more experienced sales producers (an industry term for agents who bring in premium money), along with administrative assistants (referred to as production assistants) and other support personnel. The junior team was similar in design except that its members were the more junior producers in the firm. Finally, the small accounts team was made up entirely of administrative personnel (no sales producers were included) and handled all small accounts (those that brought in annual premiums less than $500). Our primary focus is on the dynamics that occurred in the senior and junior teams following the introduction of the self-managed team system.

ORGANIZATION THEMES

The Research

Through a series of interviews, two group meetings with team members, a questionnaire, and observing the organization at work, we discovered several themes that reveal how teams were used to disempower employees.

At two *group meetings*, one for members of the senior team and one for members of the junior team, we asked, "Considering the recent change to the team system, how has the change: (a) helped you, and (b) hindered you in accomplishing what you would like to in your job?" First, team members, independently and silently, generated written lists of answers to the question. After a discussion of the combined ideas generated from all the lists, each individual privately rated each item on a scale ranging from 1 (very important) to 5 (not at all important).

Interviews were conducted with employees at all levels of the organization. First, a series of interviews was conducted with the CEO over a period of about four months. The CEO was very articulate and appeared to be open and candid, as well as highly motivated to provide complete information during the interviews. Each interview session with him lasted about two hours and was kept flexible to focus on issues that emerged during the course of the discussions. Interviews were also conducted with seven members from the senior and junior teams.

Our *observations* of the work system during each of our visits to the organization led to a better general understanding of the team system and provided valuable insights that helped us to interpret the other information we collected. Finally, we prepared a *questionnaire* based in part on information obtained from our other study methods. The questionnaire focused on such issues as employees' satisfaction, feelings of autonomy, degree of cooperation, performance, and quality of service to clients. Based on these sources, we discovered four primary themes.

Team Rationale: Self-Management—or Coordination, Efficiency, and Control?

This was the most important theme; the team concept did provide some distinct coordination and efficiency advantages. One junior team member noted that the work system "helps us to be more organized, especially for producers who do not follow procedures." Each team was expected to meet approximately once per week. Initial meetings often focused on company rules and procedures. Junior team members, in particular, told us that these first meetings had been badly needed and were quite productive. Also, given the diversity of job functions on each team (sales producers, production assistants, marketing personnel, and others) meetings provided a forum to discuss and coordinate work flow issues.

The junior team identified several organization and efficiency advantages: clarifying individual responsibility for work, developing a more uniform approach to account handling, facilitating system development and definition and understanding of responsibilities, and designating specific responsibility for special problems. The senior team identified similar issues, including providing more consistent customer service and developing greater knowledge of a smaller number of accounts. Similarly, the questionnaire indicated that the team approach made it clear who was responsible for what.

Efficiency was apparently a high priority of the acting CEO. Senior team members described him as "an efficiency man" and "the most organized man I know. He may be too organized." Junior team members indicated, "He helped me be more organized" and "Before he came, there was a low level of organization in both the people and the firm."

Over time, however, tension emerged concerning this emphasis on efficiency and organization. The agenda of team meetings continued to focus on procedural issues, a tendency apparently fostered by leaders of each team (both team leaders were administrators—a production assistant on the junior team and the marketing specialist on the senior team), whose jobs were made easier when procedures were followed closely by the producers in the team. (The team leaders were selected by the teams, but the acting CEO significantly influenced this process.)

Tension emerged concerning the emphasis on efficiency and organization.

Many individuals expressed frustration with the perceived overemphasis on procedures, indicating on the questionnaire that the new system had resulted in "unnecessary paperwork." An obvious distaste was expressed for the firm's procedural manual, which some team members described as highly detailed ("our bible"). But when we examined this manual, we discovered that it was rather brief—almost an elaborated pamphlet—and limited to a small set of apparently crucial procedural matters. We concluded that overstructuring may be in the eye of the beholder. Perhaps team members' perception of the amount of structure imposed on them was distorted by the frustration they experienced when their expectations and preferences for individual autonomy were violated.

The strong emphasis on rules and procedures in the team system appeared to threaten the sales producers' autonomy and discretion. Team members were pressured to perform a variety of activities dictated by the organization's approach rather than based on their own personal styles. For example, freedom to service small but loyal accounts—a high priority under the old system—was essentially removed. In fact, the questionnaire suggested that producers, particularly on the senior team, felt they had inadequate autonomy. The group meetings, interviews, and questionnaire responses indicated that if the company's procedures were rigidly enforced, *individual* autonomy for the producers would be very limited. The boundaries placed on self-management would be seen as so restrictive that the remaining area of discretion would be perceived as inconsequential.

In this company, self-managing teams were operating as vehicles for *limiting* autonomy. One possible conclusion is that these were not self-managing teams at all but merely traditional groups falsely labeled as "self-managing." On the other hand, the external trappings appeared quite similar in design to self-managing teams in other settings. Even so, the process that was unfolding here was in many respects limiting, rather than increasing the freedom for employees to manage themselves. Again, a major reason for this outcome may be the emphasis placed on the small-group process as a means for clarifying and enforcing rules and procedures rather than for empowering employees. Another may be the standard of comparison that the members brought to the teams. An individual's perception of autonomy is largely based on a relative, rather than absolute, standard of comparison. The producers who were members of these teams had been relatively autonomous under the old system, even though the agency itself was somewhat bureaucratic. Each producer, although not explicitly told that he was "self-managed" (all were male), was able to set his own priorities, work schedule, and the like, without first having to reach consensus with others.

In this setting, teams were seen as limiting self-management.

Interestingly, the two teams appeared to perceive the external control pressures differently. The senior team members seemed to sense the primary threat to their autonomy as stemming from having to cooperate with other team members. The senior team leader described the situation in this way: "Senior producers are on a constant ego trip. Under the team system we have a democratic ideal. This is hard work. We have several different personalities. These people don't know how to cooperate." A senior producer told us in an interview that if he could change the work system, he would return to a system of independent producers with assigned support staff. He added, "The old system was like a profit center. You could do things."

The junior team seemed to be especially frustrated with the emphasis on rules and procedures. They tended to associate control pressures more with the organization (the work system) and with the personal agenda of their leader than with their team itself. The team was, in fact, viewed more as a source of support than a constraint. One junior producer described his team as providing a place to "compare notes [to share knowledge] with others" and a mechanism for bringing "different types [producers, production assistants and marketing people] together."

The questionnaire (and our other information sources) provided support for this pattern of differences between the two teams. The junior team reported a greater feeling than the senior team of a "pressure to produce results" and "organization conformity pressure." It also reported a slightly lower "team conformity pressure."

Although these perceptual differences between teams are interesting, the primary theme remains the apparent trade-off between the self-managing team system and personal control. Most published studies of self-managing teams have dealt with occupations and situations in which the work prior to the teams was highly structured, so a change to teams caused an increase in autonomy. In many traditional manufacturing and service work settings, introduction of self-managing teams has led to substantial worker autonomy relative to the industry norm. In this organization, by contrast, the change may have been in the opposite direction. Visualize a continuum with one pole representing complete anarchy and the other total control. Somewhere in the middle range is the autonomy interdependence represented by self-managing teams. Whether teams represent autonomy to the participant depends on his or her prior location on the continuum. In this particular setting, to a large degree, team self-management was introducing a loss of personal self-management—the opposite effect of business without bosses.

Team self-management was introducing a loss of personal self-management.

Reduced Customer Service and Organizational Unity

The emphasis on work teams in the firm had two other significant impacts—a loss of agency identity and reduced customer service on small accounts—both especially troubling to senior team members.

Senior team members generally reported that the system promoted team unity, but they felt a sense of agency unity was lost. Outside their team, other sales producers would not possess the knowledge to follow up on a sales producer's accounts if he or she were absent. Team members reported that separation between units caused employees to lose sight of the whole; the system led to a loss of loyalty to the agency; no "young backups" were developed for older producers' accounts; and so forth.

Also, the separation of all small accounts into a third team—one that had no sales producers—troubled senior team members. One member put it this way: "We've lost control and communications on small accounts . . . lost our purpose of serving clients better." A major reason that this bothered some producers was that some small account personal policies were owned by key contacts for large organizational policies. One producer recounted a story in which a policyholder was given notice of cancellation of a personal policy for being a few days overdue on his premium payment. This client also happened to be the company representative on a very large corporate policy (worth hundreds of thousands of dollars). Since the personal policy was handled by administrators in the small accounts team, no special effort was made to provide special service in dealing with this problem.

Team members jointly described the problem in the senior team meeting in the following (composite) way: "The system does not go far enough. It should not split one producer's accounts. Accounts should be divided by producer, not by size. With the system we no longer manage personal accounts as a spinoff from large ones; we lose coordination. We lose brother, sister, aunt, and uncle generated by personal contact." Overall, it was clear (particularly in the senior team) that the self-managing team system was constraining a number of sales producers from servicing small accounts in the way they would if they operated on an individual basis. Here, too, the attempt at achieving efficiency and organization within the system was limiting the discretion and self-management of sales producers.

Education and Training Impacts the Level of Self-Management

Another primary theme concerned the education and training of sales producers. Both the senior and junior teams generally agreed that interaction with others enabled team members to learn from one another, a particularly important benefit for younger, less experienced sales producers. But a disadvantage of the team system was that it created roadblocks between junior producers and senior producers. There was a tendency for team members to be isolated from the activities of other teams.

In the senior team meeting, for example, two of the concerns recorded were "lose benefit of people in the other team . . . cheats inexperienced people of education" and "can't introduce young producers to senior accounts without crossing team lines." Similarly, junior producers were reluctant to go to the other team for help. As one senior producer pointed out, junior producers need "education, guidance, and motivation." His view was that the current system discouraged senior, experienced producers from helping junior people with these needs.

This concern with the education of sales producers is quite consistent with the primary focus of this chapter. The issue of personal freedom involves self-constraints as well as external constraints. The development and learning of the young, inexperienced sales producers is important for providing them with the skills and confidence necessary for effective performance. Sharing ideas and concerns with fellow inexperienced producers in a team setting was viewed as being helpful in this regard. Separation of the senior, more experienced producers, who presumably have the knowledge junior producers need, was considered by many employees to be detrimental.

Leadership Practices

The fourth theme centered on leadership practices within the work system. The issue of team leader assignments was a special concern for the junior team. The acting CEO of the firm had made his desired choice for the position known, and this person was subsequently selected by the team. The team leader was generally respected for her work ability, but her concerns did not reflect those of the majority of team members. Two different sales producers, in separate interviews, said flatly that their team leader's conduct of the meetings focused on "the production assistants' concerns" (procedures). In contrast, the production assistants thought that the team system did provide individual freedom but *too little* attention to established procedures!

The acting CEO made his desired choice for the position of team leader known.

There was a natural conflict of interest between producers and production assistants in this regard. Producers wanted freedom from the red tape of procedures, while production assistants wanted procedures to be carefully followed to reduce their own hassles. The junior team leader apparently chose to focus on this latter concern in meetings, to the dismay of producers. In the team meeting (which included the team leader), one producer said the term of a team leader is too long and should be limited to three months. This was probably as negative a response as could be made in the presence of the team leader. One producer expressed confusion and obvious irritation about how the leader got the position to begin with. Over time, the meetings became shorter and shorter and, in the eyes of most participants, nonproductive. They also became less frequent as, apparently, the incentives for attending were not sufficiently strong.

The acting CEO responded by putting pressure on the teams to be productive and by attending meetings and prodding members to participate—strikingly inconsistent with the principle of self-management and business without bosses. He took pride in his ability to get employees to do what he wanted them to do. For example, he stated, with satisfaction, he could direct his employees to participate in our study. Although he stated that participation in the study should be voluntary, his offer to make it mandatory provided an interesting contrast. Along the same lines, our interviews revealed that the "self-managing" work system itself was instituted without the participation or consent of employees. Our extensive interviews with the acting CEO led us to conclude that he was sincerely committed philosophically to employee participation, but his espoused theory was inconsistent with his theory in use.[3] This contradiction supported our general impressions of the work system: the introduction of work teams was leading to a loss of individual self-management for employees.

> The self-managing work system was instituted without the participation or consent of the employees.

As a result, senior producers, who did not need significant moral support from their peers (to develop confidence and skills), were not motivated to support the new system, and junior sales producers, who did need this moral support, were frustrated by their nonrepresentative, procedure-focused team leadership. Eventually team meetings became infrequent and nonproductive, employee skepticism and apathy regarding the team approach rose, and efficiency and coordination plummeted.

The final piece of evidence of employee feelings of reduced autonomy came from answers to our question, "How is the direction of the organization's activities established?" The responses could range from "democratically" to "autocratically." The average response was significantly above the midpoint toward "autocratically."

IMPLICATIONS FOR BUSINESS WITHOUT BOSSES

The story told in this chapter is especially interesting because it examines a setting in which an industry-wide reliance on autonomy and individual self-management is traditional. Our findings suggested a paradox: team self-management can result in a loss of individual control. Leadership practice, group peer pressure, a focus on rigid procedures, and restrictions on junior producers' exposure to experienced role models combined to undermine individual discretion and self-management.

It is important to view this chapter in the light of the uniqueness of the organizational setting. In no way do we mean to suggest that the experience of one service organization indicates that self-managing work teams are inherently threatening to personal self-management and business without bosses. This particular situation contained a number of characteristics specific to this firm and to this industry—one in which individual autonomy has been a norm. As the insurance industry has been forced to examine new ways of organizing to improve efficiency in the face of deregulation, tightening markets, and increasing competition, independent insurance salespersons have been confronted with some new restrictions on their freedom and autonomy. Against this backdrop, self-managing work teams apparently served as a convenient vehicle for increasing control over employees and for gaining some advantages in efficiency—a noteworthy challenge to the universal applicability of conventional wisdom regarding the impact of self-managing teams. In some instances, a "self-managing" team system may serve as a control mechanism that is actually more constraining than the system it replaces.

This story points to a need to understand self-managing teams in work contexts beyond manufacturing settings that have previously emphasized external control. As teams continue to spread through service and white-collar settings, we need answers to several important questions:

1. Under what conditions does the introduction of self-managing teams increase worker autonomy, and under what conditions does it reduce autonomy?

2. How do self-managing teams facilitate employee learning and development, and under what conditions do they limit it?

3. What behaviors are appropriate for self-managing team leaders, and how should their behavior vary according to work setting?

4. What results can be expected from placing self-managing teams in service organizations? How do these results contrast with those found in manufacturing settings?

5. What effect does technological interdependence have on the effectiveness of teams? Does an absence of interdependence suggest that teams may be less useful in certain settings?

6. How does the reward system influence team effectiveness? Are individual incentives inconsistent with a team philosophy?

7. What self-management alternatives capture some of the benefits of employee empowerment without introducing work teams? For example, is individual-based self-management more appropriate in some work settings?[4]

8. How can we ensure that the introduction of self-managing teams advances the objective of business without bosses? What are

some key warning signals that a team system is producing more boss control and less self-management?

Some unexpected results can occur when self-managing teams are introduced under nontraditional circumstances. If team members are not involved in establishing team responsibilities, the design of a work system that emphasizes rules and procedures can lead to oppressive boss control of work team members, especially in situations in which employees already possessed a significant amount of autonomy and self-management.

The term "self-managing team" can be badly abused.

Our final meeting with the CEO (who had become president of the organization) provided a fitting conclusion. We asked if perhaps he had really intended to use the "self-managing" teams to extend and amplify his personal influence and control. He agreed: "Every reason for doing the team system was control." At least in this executive's view, there is no inconsistency in labeling such groups "self-managing"!

The implications of this story are compelling. Depending on the objectives pursued by self-managing teams, the nature of the setting in which they are put in place, and the way that they are implemented and maintained, team-based self-management has the potential for undermining individual discretion, autonomy, and initiative. Business with more boss control, not less, can be the result.

Key Lessons for Creating Business Without Bosses

1. The reason for implementing self-managing teams is an important consideration. If the teams are intended to serve as a vehicle for enforcing company policy and procedures, individual discretion and self-management are put at risk.

2. The impact of leadership practices at both higher management levels and at the team levels will be strongly influenced by leadership agendas—for example, whether they are aimed at pursuing the concerns of management, the members, or the team leaders themselves.

3. The removal of self-constraints (e.g., skill deficiencies, low self-esteem), as well as external constraints, is important to enhance self-management. For example, provision of role models and training and learning opportunities is important for equipping employees to be effectively self-managing.

4. Incentives provided by the work system for team members to belong and to contribute constructively to their team's performance are important for work team effectiveness.

5. Recognition of the different needs of employees in different job categories (e.g , sales producers versus production assistants) is an important element of the team system design.

Chapter 6

Self–Management
Without Formal Teams:
The Organization
as Team

To make money and have fun.
—W. L. Gore

Business without bosses through teams comes in all shapes and sizes. This chapter tells the story of the highly creative and successful W. L. Gore & Associates, where teams are created as needed. The Gore recipe includes associates, not employees, who interact directly with whomever they need to get the job done rather than through a chain of command. "Unmanagement" (implying "unbosses"), "unstructure," empowerment, and self-leadership characterize this high-performing organization, which can be described as one large SuperTeam.

This chapter was written by Frank Shipper and Charles C. Manz.

W. L. Gore & Associates takes the idea of business without bosses to another level: It offers the potential to obtain many of the advantages and benefits of formally established empowered employee work teams without the formality of designated teams. Rather, the whole work operation becomes essentially one large, empowered SuperTeam where each person is individually self-managing and can interact directly with everyone else in the system. Gore relies on self-developing teams without managers or bosses but with lots of leaders.[1]

The whole organization becomes one large, empowered SuperTeam.

IN THE BEGINNING:
THE WILBERT L. GORE STORY

W. L. Gore & Associates evolved from the late Wilbert L. Gore's personal, organizational, and technical experiences. While he worked at E. I. du Pont de Nemours, he was part of a team to develop applications for polytetrafluoroethylene (PTFE), more commonly known as Teflon®. After some experimenting, he realized this material had the ideal insulating characteristics for use with computers and transistors.

He tried several ways to make a PTFE-coated ribbon cable without success. A breakthrough came in his home basement laboratory. He was explaining the problem to his son, Bob. Bob saw some PTFE sealant tape made by 3M and asked his father, "Why don't you try this tape?" His father then explained to his son that everyone knows you can not bond PTFE to itself. Bob went on to bed.

Bill Gore remained in his basement lab and proceeded to try what everyone knew would not work. At about 4 A.M., he woke up his son waving a small piece of cable, saying excitedly, "It works, it works." The following night, father and son returned to the basement lab to make ribbon cable coated with PTFE.

For the next four months, Bill Gore tried to persuade DuPont to make a new product, PTFE-coated ribbon cable. But his employer was not interested in fabricating a product (du Pont wanted to remain a supplier of raw materials), and so Gore struck out on his own.

On January 1, 1958, their twenty-third wedding anniversary, Bill and his wife, Genevieve, founded W. L. Gore & Associates in the basement of their home. After finishing their anniversary dinner, Vieve turned to her husband of 23 years and said, "Well, let's clear up the dishes, go downstairs, and get to work." They viewed this as a continuation of their partnership. Bill Gore was 45 years old with five children to support when he left du Pont. He left behind a career of 17 years, and a good and secure salary. To finance the first two years of the business they mortgaged their house and took $4,000 from savings. All of their friends told them not to do it.

The first few years were rough. In lieu of salary some of their employees accepted room and board in the Gore home. At one point eleven employees were living and working under one roof. A few years later, the Gores secured an order for $100,000 that put the company over the hump and business began to take off.

W. L. Gore & Associates has continued to grow and develop new products primarily derived from PTFE, including its best-known product, Gore-Tex. Today W. L. Gore makes a wide range of products in four categories: electronic, medical, fabrics, and industrial products. Bill Gore died in 1986 while backpacking in Wyoming. Before he died, he had become chairman and, his son, Bob, president, a position he continues to occupy. Vieve remains as the only other officer, secretary-treasurer.

THE ORGANIZATION WITHOUT BOSSES

W. L. Gore & Associates is a company without titles, hierarchy, or any of the other conventional structures typically associated with enterprises of its size. The titles of president and secretary-treasurer are used only because they are required by the laws of incorporation. The management style at Gore has been referred to as "unmanagement." The organization's development was guided by Bill's experiences on teams at du Pont and evolved over time to adapt to current needs.

In 1965, W. L. Gore & Associates was a thriving and growing company with a facility in Newark, Delaware, and about 200 employees. One morning, Bill Gore was taking his usual walk through the plant and realized that he did not know everyone there. The team, he decided, had become too big. As a result, the company developed a policy that no facility will have over 150 to 200 employees. Thus was born the expansion policy, "Get big by staying small." The purpose of maintaining small plants is to accentuate a closely knit, interpersonal atmosphere. Today W. L. Gore & Associates consists of forty-four plants worldwide (some clustered on the same site) with over 5,300 associates. For example, in Flagstaff, Arizona, Gore has four plants on the same site. Twenty-seven of those plants are in the United States and seventeen are overseas. Gore overseas plants are located in Scotland, Germany, France, Japan, and India.

The management style used at Gore has been called "unmanagement."

Compensation at W. L. Gore & Associates takes three forms: salary, profit sharing, and an associates' stock option program (ASOP).[2] Entry-level salary is in the middle of external comparable jobs. According to Sally Gore, daughter-in-law of the founder, "We do not feel we need to be the highest paid. We never try to steal people away from other companies with salary. We want them to come here because of the opportunities for growth and the unique work environment." Associates' salaries are reviewed at least once a year and more commonly twice a year. For most workers, the reviews are conducted by a compensation team from the facility in which they work. All associates have sponsors who act as their advocate during this review process. Prior to meeting with the compensation committee, the sponsor checks with customers or anyone else who uses the results of the person's work to find out what contribution has been made. In addition, the evaluation team considers the associate's leadership ability and willingness to help others to develop to their fullest.

In addition to salaries, W. L. Gore has profit-sharing and ASOP plans (similar to an ESOP plan) for all associates. Profit-sharing typically occurs twice a year (depending on profitability), with the amount awarded to each associate based on his or her time in service and annual rate of pay. In addition, the firm buys company stock equivalent to 15 percent of each associate's annual income and places it in a retirement fund. Thus, an associate becomes a stockholder after employment at Gore for one year. Bill wanted each associate to feel as if he or she was an owner.

The principle of commitment works both ways. Gore tries to avoid layoffs and cutting pay, which is considered disastrous to morale. Rather, the company has used a system of temporary transfers within a plant or cluster of plants and voluntary layoffs to cope with downturns in business.

Bill wanted each associate to feel as if he or she was an owner.

Gore is an unusual company by many standards and has also been a highly successful and profitable one for 31 years. Sales jumped from $6 million in 1969 to $660 million in 1990. This tremendous growth has been financed almost entirely without debt.

A number of features that set Gore apart from other organizations serve as lessons for other organizations that want to enjoy some of the benefits that Gore has obtained. Those benefits largely stem from its unique employee empowerment approach to managing (or un-managing) an organization.

Culture and Norms Supporting Employee Empowerment and Success

Bill Gore wanted to avoid smothering the company in thick layers of formal management, which he felt stifled individual creativity. Yet he needed a system to assist new people, to follow their progress, and to provide a way of setting compensation. Thus, the firm developed its sponsor program.

Job applicants are initially screened by personnel specialists, as in most other companies. Candidates who meet the basic criteria are then interviewed by associates. Before a person is hired, an associate must agree to be the new employee's sponsor. The sponsor takes a personal interest in the new associate's contributions, problems, and goals and serves as a coach, an advocate, and a friend. The sponsor tracks the new associate's progress, provides help and encouragement, and deals with weaknesses while building on strengths. Sponsoring is not a short-term commitment. All associates have sponsors, and many have more than one. When individuals are hired, they have a sponsor in their immediate work area. If they move to another area, they have a new sponsor in that area. As associates' responsibilities grow, they may acquire additional sponsors.

The sponsor program was devised to assist new people to get started and to follow their progress.

Because the sponsoring program looks beyond conventional views of what makes a good associate, some anomalies occur in the hiring practices. Bill Gore told the story of an 84-year-old man who applied for a job and spent five years with the company. He had 30 years of experience in the industry before joining Gore. His other associates had no problems accepting him, but the personnel computer did. It insisted that his age was 48. As in this example, the Gore system of "unmanagement" attracts individuals from diverse backgrounds and creates unique success stories.

Bill Gore described three kinds of sponsorship:

1. The sponsor who helps a new associate get started on the job or helps an associate get started on a new job (*starting sponsor*).

2. The sponsor who sees to it that the associate being sponsored gets credit and recognition for contributions and accomplishments (*advocate sponsor*).

3. The sponsor who sees to it that the associate being sponsored is fairly paid for his or her contributions to the success of the enterprise (*compensation sponsor*).

A single sponsor can perform any one or all three kinds of sponsorship.

In addition to the sponsor program, Gore associates are asked to follow four guiding principles:

1. Try to be fair.

2. Use your freedom to grow.

3. Make your own commitments and keep them.

4. Consult with other associates prior to any action that may adversely affect the reputation or financial stability of the company.

The four principles are often referred to as fairness, freedom, commitment, and waterline. (The waterline terminology is drawn from an analogy to ships. A hole in a boat above the waterline poses little danger to the vessel. A hole below the waterline puts the boat in immediate danger of sinking. In other words, associates can, and are encouraged to, make decisions on their own as long as the downside risk does not threaten the survival of the organization.)

The operating principles were put to a test in 1978. By this time, the word about the qualities of Gore-Tex were being spread throughout the recreational and outdoor markets, and production and shipment had begun in volume. At first, a few complaints were heard, then, some of the clothing started coming back, finally, a great deal of the clothing was being returned. Gore-Tex was leaking. Having high-quality waterproof products was one of the two major properties responsible for Gore-Tex's success. The company's reputation and credibility were on the line.

The four principles are fairness, freedom, commitment, and waterline.

Peter W. Gilson, who led Gore's fabric division, said of the situation, "It was an incredible crisis for us at that point. We were really starting to attract attention, we were taking off . . . and then this." Peter and a number of his associates in the next few months made a number of below-the-waterline decisions. First, research determined that certain oils in human sweat were responsible for clogging the pores in Gore-Tex and altering the surface tension of the membrane. Thus, water could pass through. They also discovered that a good washing could restore the waterproof property. At first, this solution, known as the "Ivory Snow solution," was accepted.

A single letter from "Butch," a mountain guide in the Sierras, changed the company's position. Butch wrote how he had been leading a group and, "My parka leaked and my life was in danger." As Gilson said, "That scared the hell out of us. Clearly our solution was no solution at all to someone on a mountain top." All of the products were recalled. "We bought back, at our own expense, a fortune in pipeline material. Anything that was in store, at the manufacturers, or anywhere else in the pipeline," said Gilson.

Bob Gore and other associates set out to develop a permanent solution. One month later, a second-generation Gore-Tex had been developed. Additionally, any customer who returned a leaky parka was given a replacement. The replacement program alone cost Gore roughly $4 million.

The Lattice Organization Structure

Gore has been described not only as unmanaged but also as unstructured. Bill Gore himself referred to the structure as a lattice organization (Figure 6.1), with the following primary characteristics:

1. Lines of communication are direct from person to person, with no intermediary.
2. There is no fixed or assigned authority.
3. There are no bosses, only sponsors.
4. Natural leadership is defined by followership.
5. Objectives are set by those who must make them happen.
6. Tasks and functions are organized through commitments.

The structure within the lattice is complex and evolves from interpersonal interactions, commitment to responsibility, natural leadership, and group-imposed discipline.

Bill Gore explained this structure: "Every successful organization has an underground lattice. It's where the news spreads like lightning, where people can go around the organization to get things done." Another description is that the lattice structure is characterized by the constant formation of temporary cross-area groups; there are teams similar to quality circles going on all the time, but they are not formally designated. The cross-level and cross-functional interpersonal accessibility created by this structure enables teams to form in response to specific needs. Associates can team up with other associates, regardless of area, to get the job done.

Associates can team up with other associates, regardless of area, to get the job done.

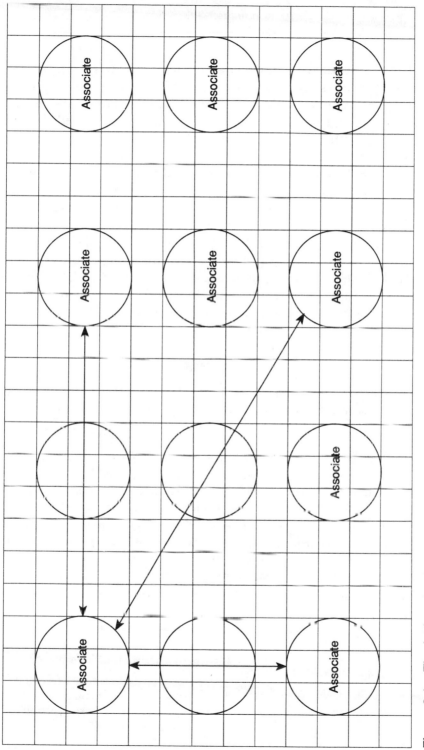

Figure 6.1. The lattice structure.

The lattice structure does have some similarities to traditional management structures. For instance, a group of 30 to 40 associates who make up an advisory group meets every six months to review marketing, sales, and production plans. As Bill Gore has conceded, "The abdication of titles and rankings can never be 100%."

An outsider observing the meetings and other activities will no doubt notice the informality and humor with these groups, but words such as "responsibilities" and "commitments" are frequently used. This is an organization in which members take what they do seriously, but not themselves.

For a company of its size, W. L. Gore may have the shortest organizational pyramid found anywhere. The pyramid consists of Bob Gore, the late Bill Gore's son, as president and Vieve, Bill Gore's widow, as secretary-treasurer. All the other members of the Gore organization are referred to as associates. Words such as employees, subordinates, and managers are taboo in the Gore culture.

Leaders

Gore has no managers but many leaders. Bill Gore once described in an internal memo the kinds of leaders who are needed and the role that they play:

1. The Associate who is recognized by a team as having a special knowledge, or experience (for example, this could be a chemist, computer expert, machine operator, salesman, engineer, lawyer). This kind of leader gives the team *guidance in a special area.*

2. The Associate the team looks to for coordination of individual activities in order to achieve the agreed upon objectives of the team. The role of this leader is to persuade team members to *make the commitments* necessary for success (commitment seeker).

3. The Associate who proposes necessary objectives and activities and seeks agreement and team *consensus on objectives.* This leader is perceived by the team members as having a good grasp of how the objectives of the team fit in with the broad objective of the enterprise. This kind of leader is often also the "commitment seeking" leader in 2 above.

4. The leader who evaluates relative contribution of team members (in consultation with other sponsors), and reports these contribu-

tion evaluations to a compensation committee. This leader may also participate in the compensation committee on relative contribution and pay and *reports changes in compensation* to individual Associates. This leader is then also a compensation sponsor.

5. The leader who coordinates the research, manufacturing and marketing of one product type within a business, interacting with team leaders and individual Associates who have commitments regarding the product type. These leaders are usually called *product specialists*. They are respected for their knowledge and dedication to their products.

6. *Plant leaders* who help coordinate activities of people within a plant.

7. *Business leaders* who help coordinate activities of people in a business.

8. *Functional leaders* who help coordinate activities of people in a "functional" area.

9. *Corporate leaders* who help coordinate activities of people in different businesses and functions and who try to promote communication and cooperation among all Associates.

10. *Intrapreneuring Associates* who *organize new teams* for new businesses, new products, new processes, new devices, new marketing efforts, new or better methods of all kinds. These leaders invite other Associates to "sign up" for their project.

It is clear that leadership is widespread in our lattice organization and that it is continually changing and evolving. The reality that leaders are frequently *also* sponsors should not confuse the fact that these are different activities and responsibilities. Leaders are not authoritarians, managers of people, or supervisors who tell us what to do or forbid us from doing things; nor are they "parents" to whom we transfer our own self-responsibility. However, they do often advise us of the consequences of actions we have done or propose to do. Our actions result in contributions, or lack of contribution, to the success of our enterprise. Our pay depends on the magnitude of our contributions. This is the basic discipline of our lattice organization.

Many other aspects are arranged along similar lines. The parking lot contains no reserved parking spaces except for customers and the disabled. There is only one area in each plant in which to eat. The lunchroom in each new plant is designed to be a focal point for employee interaction. Dave McCarter of Phoenix explains, "The design is no accident. The lunchroom in Flagstaff has a fireplace in the middle. We want people to like to be here." The location of the plant is also no accident. Sites are selected based on transportation access, a nearby university, beautiful surroundings, and climate appeal. Land cost is never a primary consideration. McCarter justifies the selection by stating, "Expanding is not costly in the long-run. The loss of money is what you make happen by stymieing people into a box."

"We want people to like to be here."

Gore's leadership approach focuses on empowering and enabling others to perform on their own and to the best of their ability. In a sense, the only real bosses for Gore employees are themselves. Gore promotes the development of creative, innovative self-leaders through SuperLeadership (leading others to lead themselves) in a total organization SuperTeam.

Working Without Structure and Management

Not all people function well under such a system, especially newcomers. Those accustomed to a structured work environment may face adjustment problems. As Bill Gore said, "All our lives most of us have been told what to do, and some people don't know how to respond when asked to do something—and have the very real option of saying no—on their job. It's the new associate's responsibility to find out what he or she can do for the good of the operation."

The vast majority of new associates may flounder initially but usually adapt quickly. For those who require more structured working conditions and cannot adapt, Gore's flexible workplace is not for them. According to Bill for those few, "It's an unhappy situation, both for the associate and the sponsor. If there is no contribution, there is no paycheck."

Ron Hill, an associate in Newark, has pointed out that the company "will work with associates who want to advance themselves." Associates are offered many in-house training opportunities. They do tend to be technical and engineering focused because of the type of organization it is, but it also offers in-house programs in leadership development. In addition, the company has cooperative programs with associates to obtain training through universities and other outside providers. Gore covers most of the costs for the associates, but the associate must take the initiative.

Anita McBride, an associate in Phoenix, realizes that Gore is "not for everybody. People ask me, Do we have turnover, and yes, we do have turnover. What you're seeing looks like utopia, but it also looks extreme. If you finally figure out the system, it can be real exciting. If you can't handle it, you gotta go—probably by your own choice, because you're going to be so frustrated."

In rare cases an associate, "tries to be unfair," as Bill put it. Such "unfairness" might involve chronic absenteeism or stealing. "When that happens, all hell breaks loose," said Bill Gore. "We can get damned authoritarian when we have to."

"If you finally figure out the system, it can be exciting."

Over the years, Gore has faced several unionization drives. It neither tries to dissuade an associate from attending an organizational meeting nor retaliates when flyers are passed out. Each attempt has been unsuccessful. Bill believed that no need exists for third-party representation under the lattice structure. He asked, "Why would associates join a union when they own the company? It seems rather absurd."

Being an associate at Gore can be a unique and challenging experience. Consider Jack Dougherty's experience. Dougherty, a newly minted M.B.A. from the College of William and Mary, bursting with resolve and dressed in a dark blue suit, reported to his first day at W. L. Gore. He presented himself to Bill Gore, shook hands firmly, looked him in the eye, and said he was ready for anything. Gore replied, "That's fine, Jack, fine. Why don't you look around and find something you'd like to do." Three frustrating weeks later, he found something. He was dressed in jeans, loading fabric into the maw of a machine that laminates Gore-Tex, the company's patented fabric, to other fabrics.

Sixteen years later, Jack had become responsible for all advertising and marketing in the fabrics group.

This story is part of Gore's folklore. Today the process is slightly more structured. New associates take a journey through the business before settling into their own positions, regardless of the specific position for which they are hired. A new sales associate in the fabric division may spend six weeks rotating through different areas before beginning to concentrate on sales and marketing. Among other things he or she may learn is how Gore-Tex is made, what it can and cannot do, how Gore handles customer complaints, and how it makes its investment decisions. Anita McBride related her early experience at W. L. Gore this way:

> "When I first came to Gore I had worked for a structured organization. I came here, and for the first month it was fairly structured because I was going through training. 'This is what we do, and this is how Gore is' and all of that, and I went to Flagstaff for that training. After a month I came down to Phoenix, and my sponsor said, 'Well, here's your office,' it's a wonderful office, and 'Here's your desk,' and walked away. And I thought, Now what do I do, you know? I was waiting for a memo or something, or a job description. Finally, after another month, I was so frustrated, I felt, What have I gotten myself into? I went to my sponsor and I said, 'What the heck do you want from me? I need something from you,' and he said, 'If you don't know what you're supposed to do, examine your commitments and opportunities.' "

Anita did find something to do; she heads up the personnel function in Phoenix.

Unstructured Research and Development

Like everything else at Gore, research and development is unstructured. There is no formal research and development department, yet the company holds over 150 patents. Most inventions are held as proprietary or trade secrets. Any associate can ask for a piece of raw PTFE, known as a silly worm, to experiment with. Bill Gore believed that all people have it within themselves to be creative.

The best way to understand how research and development works at Gore is through an example. By 1969, Gore's wire and cable division was facing increased competition, so Bill Gore began to look for a way to straighten out the PTFE molecules, the way, he thought, to "a tremendous new kind of material." If PTFE could be stretched, air could be introduced into its molecular structure. The result would be greater volume per pound of raw material without affecting performance. Thus, fabricating costs would be reduced—and profit margins increased. Going about his search in a scientific manner with his son, Bob, the Gores heated rods of PTFE to various temperatures and then slowly stretched them. Regardless of the temperature or how carefully they stretched them, the rods broke. Working alone late one night in 1969 after countless failures, Bob yanked at one of the rods violently. To his surprise, it did not break. He tried it again and again, with the same results. The next morning Bob demonstrated his breakthrough to his father, but not without some drama. As Bill Gore recalled, "Bob wanted to surprise me so he took a rod and stretched it slowly. Naturally, it broke. Then he pretended to get mad. He grabbed another rod and said, 'Oh the hell with this,' and gave it a pull. It didn't break . . . he'd done it." The new arrangement of molecules changed not only the wire and cable division but led to the development of Gore-Tex and a host of other products.

Bill Gore believed that all people had it within themselves to be creative.

Initial field-testing of Gore-Tex was conducted by Bill and his wife, Vieve, in the summer of 1970. Vieve made a hand-sewn tent out of patches of Gore-Tex. They took it on their annual camping trip to the Wind River Mountains in Wyoming. The first night out, hail tore holes in the top of the tent, but the bottom filled up like a bathtub from the rain. As Bill Gore stated, "At least we knew from all the water that the tent was waterproof. We just need to make it stronger, so it could withstand hail."

145

The second largest division began on the ski slopes: Bill was out with a friend, Ben Eiseman, a surgeon at the Denver General Hospital. As they were just about to start a run, Bill Gore remembered, "I absent-mindedly pulled a small tubular section of Gore-Tex out of my pocket and looked at it. 'What is that stuff?' Ben asked. So I told him about its properties. 'Feels great,' he said. 'What do you use it for?' 'Got no idea," I said. 'Well, give it to me,' he said, 'and I'll try it in a vascular graft on a pig.' Two weeks later, he called me up. Ben was pretty excited. 'Bill,' he said, 'I put it in a pig, and it works. What do I do now?' I told him to get together with Pete Cooper in our Flagstaff plant, and let them figure it out." Now hundreds of thousands of people throughout the world walk around with Gore-Tex vascular grafts.

Every associate is encouraged to think, experiment, and follow a potentially profitable idea to its conclusion. At a plant in Newark, Delaware, a machine that wraps thousands of yards of wire a day was designed over a weekend by Fred L. Eldreth, an associate with a third-grade education. Many other associates have contributed their ideas through both product and process breakthroughs.

Innovation and creativity work very well at Gore, even without a research and development department. The year before he died, Bill Gore claimed that "the creativity, the number of patent applications and innovative products is triple" that of du Pont. Overall, the associates appear to have responded positively to the Gore system of un-management and unstructure. Bill Gore estimated the year before he died that "the profit per associate is double" that of du Pont.

Use With Caution: Un-Management and Un-Structure Have Limitations

While the lattice structure and the unstructured management approach used at Gore appears to be a remarkable and promising organizational innovation, it should be considered with some caution. Just like any other new system, it should be evaluated in terms of its fit with the organization, its culture, and its objectives.

Bill Gore stated, "I'm told from time to time that a lattice organization can't meet a crisis well because it takes too long to reach a consensus when there are no bosses. But this isn't true. Actually, a lattice, by its very nature works particular well in a crisis. A lot of useless effort is avoided because there is no rigid management hierarchy to conquer before you can attack a problem."

The lattice has been put to the test on many occasions. For example, in 1975, Charles Campbell, the University of Pittsburgh's senior resident, reported that a Gore-Tex arterial graft had developed an aneurysm, a bubblelike protrusion that is life threatening; if it continues to expand, it will explode. Obviously, this kind of problem has to be solved quickly and permanently.

Within a few days of Dr. Campbell's first report, he flew to Newark to present his findings to Bill and Bob Gore and a few other associates. Bill Hubis, a former policeman who had joined Gore to develop new production methods, had an idea before the meeting was over. He returned to his work area to try some different production techniques. After only three hours and 12 tries, he had developed a permanent solution. In three hours, a potentially damaging problem to both patients and the company was resolved. Furthermore, Hubis's redesigned graft went on to win widespread acceptance in the medical community.

Other critics have been outsiders who had problems with the idea of no titles. Sarah Clifton, an associate at the Flagstaff facility, was being pressed by some outsiders as to what her title was. She made one up and had it printed on some business cards: "Supreme Commander." When Bill Gore learned what she did, he loved it and recounted the story to others.

One critic, Eric Reynolds, founder of Marmot Mountain Works Ltd. of Grand Junction, Colorado, and a major Gore customer, thinks "the lattice has its problems with the day-to-day nitty-gritty of getting things done on time and out the door. I don't think Bill realizes how the lattice system affects customers. I mean, after you've established a relationship with someone about product quality, you can call up one day and suddenly find that someone new to you is handling your problem. It's frustrating to find a lack of continuity." Nevertheless, "I have to admit that I've personally seen at Gore remarkable examples of people coming out of nowhere and excelling."

Critics had problems with the idea of no titles.

Bill Gore thought that "established companies would find it very difficult to use the lattice. Too many hierarchies would be destroyed. When you remove titles and positions and allow people to follow who they want, it may very well be someone other than the person who has been in charge. The lattice works for us, but it's always evolving. You have to expect problems." He maintained that the lattice system works best in start-up companies by dynamic entrepreneurs.

SUMMARY AND CONCLUSIONS

In their quest to meet a variety of significant challenges and pressures—international competition and a rapidly changing work force and business environment, among others—contemporary organizations have experimented with a variety of organizational approaches. The approach we described in this chapter features no permanent work teams and no managers. The lattice structure and "unmanagement" at Gore might be thought of as a self-developing team approach without bosses. With the lattice structure, all Gore employees interact directly with all other organizational members. In a sense the entire organization becomes one empowered interacting work SuperTeam. In addition, a variety of temporary and fluid teams spring up to address specific projects and issues. The Gore approach is a remarkable alternative to a more formalized work team approach.

Key Lessons for Creating Business Without Bosses

1. The role of management and leadership needs to be redefined. A perspective that recognizes the role of self-leadership for each employee is at the heart of this empowerment approach. At Gore they talk about "unmanagement," with no bosses or managers but with lots of leaders. Leaders emerge where they are needed, and people develop into dynamic self-leaders.

2. Organizing and structure need to be redefined as well. A concrete chain of command and definite hierarchy are not characteristics that describe W. L. Gore. Gore has only two officer positions (president and secretary-treasurer)—and those only because of requirements of the laws of incorporation. Everyone else is an associate, with no assigned title. At Gore they talk about "unstructure," not structure. The lattice allows all associates to interact directly with anyone else in the system without concern about going through a formal chain of command.

3. Some of the void that is left by lack of structure and management, in a traditional sense, can be filled by culture and norms. Gore relies on sponsors, not managers, to help guide and serve as an advocate for less experienced employees. Innovation, teamwork, and independent effort are valued, and the associates are well aware of it. The Gore culture encourages fairness, freedom, and commitments in an overall system that emphasizes contribution to the entire organizational team.

4. While formal, relatively permanent teams may not be needed, lots of teamwork is. Gore relies heavily on fluid, self-developing temporary teams and an overall commitment to contributing to the entire organization team.

5. An unstructured system that emphasizes freedom and requires individual initiative can be a difficult transition for some employees. At Gore many of the employees love the system. Those who do not, depart. Realistic job previews for applicants and orientation and training to prepare new employees to deal with high levels of autonomy are essential ingredients for organizations considering a similar system.

6. Leaving research and development unstructured while encouraging everyone to get involved can foster innovation. At Gore, everyone is encouraged to experiment with new ideas. Some of Gore's most important products have resulted from the ideas of "regular" workers who came up with a different idea and had the encouragement and freedom to follow through.

7. Consider the Gore system with caution. While W. L. Gore has achieved some impressive results, critics have pointed out potential flaws with the system. Bill Gore argued that the lattice system should work best in start-up companies with dynamic entrepreneurs. We believe many of the principles underlying the Gore system could be adopted in most organizations but should not be adopted blindly. Relying on self-developing teams without managers may not represent the right organizational approach for all, but it is worth a look.

8. Consider the notion of the total organization as team. The lattice metaphor is the structure that makes this radical idea feasible.

Chapter 7

Teams and Total Quality Management: An International Application

This chapter describes the implementation of self-managing teams as the final stage of a comprehensive total quality management program. The original organizational structure of Texas Instruments Malaysia (TIM) was a more traditional functional/vertical hierarchy, with separate specialized departments. It initiated a long-term change in 1980, centered on total quality management. Implementation of self-managing teams is the most recent phase. As a result, the worker-to-supervisor ratio went from 60:1 to 200:1, and supervisor positions have decreased from 79 to 18. Productivity continually increased while the work force size remained relatively constant. Overall, the story demonstrates how teams can play a key role in total quality management programs and that teams can provide impressive payoffs for organizations outside the United States.

This chapter was written by Alan B. Cheney, Henry P. Sims, Jr., and Charles C. Manz.

At a place most North Americans can't locate on a world map, on the other side of the world from us, just north of the equator, lies a bustling city of 1.2 million people. In the streets one can hear a variety of languages, the most common being Chinese, Tamil, Bahasa Malaysia, and English. (Many people in Kuala Lumpur speak very good English.)

This city is the setting for the story of this chapter, a story about a company that has evolved over the years from a traditional management structure to TQM (total quality management) to self-managing work teams. It's a story of how teams and TQM can be used together to conduct business without bosses. (TQM, of course, is a philosophy and set of practices intended to improve the quality of an organization's products and/or services.)

Kuala Lumpur also has a marvel that is not on many tourist itineraries, but which people, including the authors, have flown as many as 23 hours by jet to see. The semiconductor plant of Texas Instruments Malaysia Sdn. Bhd. is located in the business park called Ampang/Ulu Klang, near the zoo. The plant is one of the best examples in the world of the planned integration of self-managing work teams into a TQM environment. At this plant, TQM is the main vehicle in the transition to business without bosses.

THE COMPANY: TEXAS INSTRUMENTS MALAYSIA

Texas Instruments established a wholly owned subsidiary, Texas Instruments Malaysia (TIM), in November 1972 on a 15-acre site near Kuala Lumpur. The 250,000-square-foot facility was built to produce integrated circuits for use in computers and related products. Twenty years later, it produces about 3 million high-volume integrated circuits each day, many of which are shipped to companies in Japan. TIM employs 2,600 people, all but a handful Malaysian nationals.

Malaysia is a good place for multinational companies to do business (see the box). In addition to a favorable business climate, the Malaysian work force tends to be well educated, hard working, loyal, and dedicated to quality. Apparently the attraction is mutual. Results of TIM's annual employee attitude survey, in which ninety-seven percent participated, show an overall favorable percentage of 89.2 in 1991 and 85.3 in 1989. This represents the highest favorable percentage of all Texas Instruments plants in East Asia and one of the highest worldwide.

The positive atmosphere and mutual respect are evident at the plant. The employees smile and greet visitors, even on the plant floor. The cafeteria, which features indoor stalls selling foods from Malaysia's three major ethnic cultures (Malays, Chinese, and Tamil), is often adorned with banners celebrating holidays. There are frequent after-hours celebrations, such as family dinners recognizing company service anniversaries, the annual recreation committee ball, and the annual sports day. Employee quality awards are frequently given, and an excellent company magazine, *Gema TIM*, appears bimonthly. The company is also active as corporate citizen, from sponsorship of the Malaysian Young Enterprise Program to blood drives.

The Malaysian Economy

Malaysia is one of the world's fastest-growing economies, posting a 10 percent rise in real gross domestic product in 1991. Like other East Asian newly industrialized countries, Malaysia is friendly to business and leaves little of its economic growth to chance. It attracts multinational corporations with its political stability and 10-year government plans for improving its physical and human resources. In 1990 Prime Minister Mahathir Mohamad's government announced 2020 Vision, which details Malaysia's plan for becoming a fully developed nation by 2020. Among other things, the plan proposes that manufacturing continue to be the primary means of economic growth by being the major vehicle for export earnings. It also proposes a broadening of Malaysia's industrial base beyond electronics and textiles, which now dominate it. For example, Malaysia is now the world's third largest producer of computer chips, behind only the United States and Japan. Texas Instruments was a relatively early foreign player in contemporary Malaysia; now foreign investment capital is pouring into the economy, much of it from North Asian companies. The Malaysian-American Electronics Industry Association represents 15 American manufacturers located in Malaysia

---

Much of TIM's atmosphere and success can be linked to Jerry W. Lee, the managing director. One of his contributions has been a dedicated focus on total quality and employee involvement.

153

THE EVOLUTION OF TIM'S ORGANIZATIONAL STRUCTURE

The TIM work force is relatively mature, with 60 percent having more than 10 years of service. With cost improvement and "delayering," the organization will continue to change in the direction of a flatter structure. Thus, the future holds diminished opportunity for traditional organizational advancement up the ladder. In addition, Malaysia's booming economy and industrialization is projected to yield a shortage of experienced professionals in the labor market.

The aggregate meaning of all of these factors is that TIM has been seeking a way to provide internal achievement opportunities for employees, while improving their skills and qualifications. The TIM response has been to push responsibility to the lowest level. The story of how they have done this is the theme of this chapter. Jerry Lee calls this "building the flexible organization."

The TIM response has been to push responsibility to the lowest level.

The evolution of the form of organizational structure at TIM started in 1972. The baseline, or originating structure of the plant, was the traditional functional/vertical hierarchy, characterized by separate and specialized departments and attitudes that can be described as protectionist and ("cover your rear"). The plant remained organized in this way until 1980 and the beginning of what is now referred to as the "Eleven Year Search." (Figure 7.1 outlines the evolution of TIM's organizational structures.)

In 1980 Mohd Azmi Abdullah read about and began to discuss with others Peter Drucker's concepts of worker self-management.[1] Particularly interesting to the TIM managers were Drucker's three prerequisites for self-management: productive work, continuous feedback enabling self-direction, and a continuous learning environment. Mohd Azmi Abdullah remembers, "We thought, 'This looks very good, but how do you apply it?' We couldn't find any methodology to do it, so we weren't able to try it then." But a seed was planted.

By 1982, TIM's structure had evolved to a matrix form, characterized by an intertwining of the traditional vertical organization with

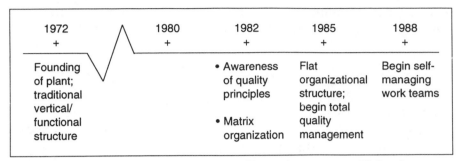

Figure 7.1. Organizational changes at Texas Instruments Malaysia.

project management. This matrix structure was distinguished by the typical conflict between project management needs and the vertical hierarchy. Three years later, TIM was swept up in what was becoming a worldwide phenomenon: the discovery of and emphasis on total quality. At that time, the perspectives of Deming and Juran were most influential. The story of these two pioneers, of their initial rejection in the United States and embrace in Japan, is well known and we won't rehash it here. It is important to note, however, that at TI Malaysia, perspectives and contributions from both U.S. and Japanese management have always been considered and evaluated with some interest—perhaps because of Japan's geographical and cultural proximity.

The aim is to involve employees in ways to improve quality and cut costs.

Since 1980, total quality has been a focus of Texas Instruments worldwide. In a company brochure called Management Perspective: Customer Satisfaction Through Total Quality, chairman, president, and CEO Jerry R. Junkins writes, "Over the past few years, we have changed our culture within TI to focus on Total Quality. Today, this concept is well-established and the essentials of guaranteeing customer satisfaction are in place, but we must realize Total Quality is a continuous process and our journey along this path is never-ending." At Texas Instruments, the three components of customer satisfaction through total quality are: customer focus, continuous improvement, and people involvement. Junkins writes, "More than any other factor, dedicated TIers contributing ideas through teamwork is vital to our continued success." This commitment to total quality by the parent corporation was an important backdrop to the change at TIM.

QUALITY IMPROVEMENT TEAMS AND EFFECTIVENESS TEAMS

Among Juran's ideas, those addressing operator self-control especially captured the attention of Mohd Azmi Abdullah. Like Drucker, Juran stressed prerequisites to increased employee participation: a knowledge of what one is supposed to do, the ability to monitor one's own performance, and the ability to regulate one's own activities through a decision-making process. Juran also proposed a model for building self-control into operations. At TIM, his ideas found form in quality circles[2] and their close relative, quality improvement teams, all designed to involve employees in ways to improve quality and cut costs.

Quality improvement teams, which form to resolve specific problems or issues, started in the management and engineering offices. The reason, Mohd Azmi explains, is that "according to Dr. Juran, 80 percent or more of problems are management-controllable problems. For example, many systems, design, and other problems are not operator controllable." The first quality improvement teams consisted of managers and professionals from different departments; they were cross-functional. A QIT team might be formed to look at reducing cycle time. The manufacturing manager, appointed to form the team, would recruit members from other departments—accounting, planning, production, facilities, and so forth. By forming quality improvement teams in this way, departmental barriers began to break down. Eventually, breaking down interdepartmental barriers led to the actual removal of physical barriers. Today at TIM, individuals representing all functions—assemblers, process engineers, manufacturing engineers, planners, and equipment engineers—sit together in a common area.

Following the success of quality improvement teams at the management and professional support levels, effectiveness teams (quality circles) were created among workers. Made up of employees from the same work area, they met regularly to solve specific quality, productivity, and customer service problems. Sometimes viewed as a precursor to self-managing work teams, quality circles have contributed to several important paradigm shifts for companies that have used them successfully. Among these contributions are a realization of the value of worker input into solving work-related problems, the value of cross-functional (interdepartmental or across-jobs) problem solving, and a clear demonstration of how involved and committed most workers will become when invited into the decision-making process.

As in other companies that sponsor quality circles, TIM employees are encouraged to form effectiveness teams among themselves. A team leader is selected and trained. Then each team selects a work-related problem as a project and meets regularly to discuss it, following a problem-solving methodology. The team eventually devises recommendations to solve the problem and makes a formal presentation to the plant management.

One effectiveness team from TIM's solder dip function (one of the steps in making semiconductors) has nine members—technicians and expediters. They work on different shifts but still manage to meet weekly to work on their project. Their first project, which solved a difficult production problem, won an incentive award. For their second project, they chose to look for ways to improve a process called the solder pot crank system. Again their recommended changes were implemented, solving another production problem and saving the company more time and money. Again, team members were given an incentive award (an all-expenses-paid weekend trip), were written up in *Gema TIM*, and made a presentation. The team leader Lien S.S. had this to say: "ET [the effectiveness team] has given us the opportunity to solve our work problem and made our work much easier. We also learned to solve problems systematically, which we were never taught in school. It brings us together as one family working for a common objective. Our communication has improved. We understand each other, and there is better cooperation and, best of all, we are recognized!"

"It brings us together as one common family working for a common objective."

One of the major vehicles for learning to solve problems systematically is the "QC [quality circle] Story," a problem-solving procedure used extensively in Japan. Following are the steps usually employed in a QC Story:

1. Selecting a theme (problem); includes reasons why the quality circle chose the problem, a Pareto diagram (which shows key factors contributing to the problem), and specific goals for the team's activities.

2. Understanding the situation. Team members use SPC (statistical process controls) tools such as histograms and cause-and-effect diagrams to analyze the problem and identify variances in quality.

3. Setting the target. Specific improvement targets (goals) and target dates are set based on available data.

4. Analyzing factors contributing to the problem and applying countermeasures to enable the quality circle members to attain their target.

5. Measuring results. Tangible results, such as decreased or eliminated variances in quality, are reported, as are intangible results, such as an increase in realization by workers of the importance of daily quality controls or improved quality procedures.

6. Developing measures to prevent backsliding. Team members develop countermeasures aimed at preventing any recurrence of the problem. Procedure manuals are often created or updated in order to standardize the improvements.

7. Developing insights and looking to future directions, a concept summed up as *kaizen*.

Because of the positive response to effectiveness teams, in December 1989, a council was formed to coordinate team activities and promote expansion of the program. The council is responsible for providing support and encouragement to individual teams, coordinating training for team leaders and members, and providing guidance as necessary to ensure completion of team projects. The council plans to create a resource center with audiovisual equipment and reading material, foster awards for teams completing their projects, and organize rallies for team members and an annual convention. Effectiveness teams that complete their projects are recognized in the TIM magazine and can present their projects at the annual TI Malaysia/TI Singapore ET Presentation.

QUALITY AT THE SOURCE

The QC Story is just one of the tools TIM employees use. Beginning in 1985, TIM managers began to put operator self-control into practice. First, they taught operators how to recognize problems and arrive at solutions; then they gave them the responsibility, discretion, and authority to implement the solutions.

Extensive training was begun to give operators the knowledge and skills needed to monitor their own work, to look for and recognize variances in quality, and to know what to do when they saw problems. In many cases, this training simply polished or standardized existing worker skills. TIM, like most other companies, had been set up in a line manufacturing format, with each operator on the line performing a specific job. At the end of the production line, quality control inspectors, in a separate function, were responsible for catching quality problems. Workers on the line were not encouraged, or even allowed, to point out problems they saw. That was the job of highly trained QC inspectors. Stories abound all over the world of line workers, "not paid to think," quietly watching defective materials go down the line. Sometimes it even became a game: "Will the QC inspectors catch that piece of junk? Ha! They missed it!" As a result, quality, and the customer, often suffered.

At the beginning, inspectors were responsible for catching quality problems.

Juran had declared that three requirements had to be met if operator self-control was to work. The first, a knowledge of what one is supposed to do, was accomplished at TIM by expanding the job of each operator to include monitoring the quality of his or her own work. Quality awareness training was given, and job descriptions were changed to promote quality at the source.

Juran's second prerequisite, the ability to monitor one's own performance, was accomplished through training that provided knowledge and skills in quality inspection and control. Statistical process control techniques, developed in the 1950s in Japan, were taught to line operators, and tools such as Pareto analyses, control charts, fishbone or cause-and-effect diagrams, and run charts were introduced.

The third requirement, the ability to regulate one's own activities through a decision-making process, was taught through the use of Deming's PDCA (Plan-Do-Check-Act) cycle, the QC Story, and other frameworks for problem solving and decision making. The QC inspectors did all this training. As a result, after much of the training was accomplished, a sizable number of QC jobs were eliminated. The people who had formerly performed those jobs were given new responsibilities at the plant, since the QC function had become an integral part of each operator's job.

Operators were empowered to act.

After operators were taught the principles and tools of quality at the source, they were empowered to practice them. A major aspect of empowerment is the authority to act on decisions. At TIM, operators are allowed to shut down the line when a defect is found. Previously, only QC inspectors had this authority by formally writing out a machine shutdown tag.

SELF-MANAGING WORK TEAMS AS A TOTAL QUALITY TOOL

TIM is now using self-managing work teams as an integral component of their evolution into a TQM culture. Mohd Azmi says, "All quality activities here are aimed at trying to satisfy customers. Customers look at quality, cost, service, and so forth. But at TIM, people development shares equal priority with customer satisfaction. Why? If our people are not developed and trained to deliver, you cannot have customer satisfaction. Personal development is the cause and customer satisfaction is the effect or result." Employees are quite proud of their ability to satisfy the rigorous quality requirements of their Japanese customers. Mohd Azmi says, "It is not easy to penetrate the Japanese market. They'll come and audit you for months. They'll go out and inspect the road to your factory and if they find a cigarette butt, they'll chew you out, saying, 'You think your people can produce quality products, and they have no discipline!' We listen to them, though, and make a lot of

The Quality Garden (Shrine)

The Texas Instruments Malaysian plant is located in an exotic setting compared to the other locations we describe in this book. Kuala Lumpur, with its lush tropical plants and rich cultural diversity, creates a fascinating backdrop for self-managing teams. The large industrial complex itself, however, at first seems similar to a thousand other production facilities. There are several buildings with a factory-setting appearance interwoven with paved parking lots filled with rows of employee cars. Inside, a honeycomb of work rooms are bustling with production activity. Off the long hallways are meeting rooms, restrooms, drinking fountains, and many company displays, all contributing to the familiar feel of a factory, albeit a very clean, orderly one.

A visitor who entered through a particular main factory entrance into this production environment could easily overlook a small garden area immediately to the right of the door. This well-kept garden features a beautiful display of carefully arranged native tropical plants, creating a natural picture that is visually pleasing to the eye.

At the center of the garden is a small stone-looking structure that appears to be a compact monument of some kind. It is the plant's quality shrine—a continual reminder and symbol of TIM's commitment to quality. The garden is a particularly appropriate symbol of the total quality emphasis at TIM. The garden and the stone form a natural blending of numerous living organisms to create a total quality product. It represents in a creative and powerful way the dedication to total quality.

improvements." All over the TIM facility are brass plates with the word KAIZEN. Here, however, they try to make continuous improvement more than a slogan. Another striking symbol of the commitment to total quality can be found near one of the main entrances to the plant. It is the Quality Garden, a lush and attractive garden surrounding a marble monument on which is inscribed TIM's commitment to TQM. (See the box above.) We were told that Japanese visitors are especially impressed by this beautiful and constant reminder.

After redesigning the work to integrate quality at the source, TIM managers went on in 1989 to begin implementing what they call the flexible organization. The design of the flexible organization has three components: a quality steering team (the plant manager and his reports), a process management team (middle managers and engineers, chartered with providing guidance and expertise), and self-managing work teams. These three groups have two basic functions in common: Maintain and Improve, the two pillars of continuous improvement. Following Juran's model, the Maintain function guarantees the maintenance of processes, actively looks for problem situations, monitors quality, and promotes total participation. The Improve function embodies KAIZEN, the continuous improvement of work standards and quality. "Hold the gain—improve—hold the gain—improve."

TIM is proud of its ability to satisfy the rigorous quality requirements of Japanese customers.

To begin moving toward self-managing work teams, TIM first instituted total productive maintenance, another concept developed in Japan, that attempts to maximize equipment effectiveness with a total system of preventive maintenance covering the entire life of the equipment. People are motivated to achieve this result through small-group and voluntary activities. Like quality at the source, it is designed to include workers as more than mere operators of equipment; they are charged with maintaining the working order of their own equipment. And as with quality at the source, where the work of quality control inspectors is largely replaced by the workers themselves, total productive maintenance takes routine maintenance responsibility from a maintenance department and places it on the machine operators.

Several steps are required to set up this concept. First, machine operators learn to clean their machines using standard cleaning procedures. Next, they learn to adjust the machine when something goes wrong. Previously they were instructed to stop a machine with even small maladjustments and tell their supervisor. The supervisor then filled out a maintenance request order, which was sent to Maintenance and answered perhaps the next day (or later!). Although many seasoned operators knew how to perform these minor adjustments, they were not permitted to do so.

In the next step, workers learn to clean and oil their machines. Then they become responsible for total inspection of the machine operation using the manual, which is followed by preventive maintenance. They learn in detail how each machine operation affects the quality of their product. Finally, each operator becomes responsible for total preventive maintenance. Generally the full process takes three years.

TIM's V. P. Murugan explains, "In the early days, a machine was repaired only after it broke down. Then time-based preventive maintenance was introduced. That was further improved by the addition of condition monitoring and reliability engineering. Total productive maintenance is productive maintenance involving total participation. Its success depends on everyone's cooperation and participation." According to Murugan, the advantages of total productive maintenance are increased productivity through the elimination of equipment losses, better quality, a minimum inventory of spare parts, zero pollution, a safe working environment through elimination of accidents, and a pleasant working environment. At TIM, a particular method, the Five S's, is used. Each S represents a Japanese word and component of involvement: *Seiri* ("cleaning"), *Seiton* ("tidiness"), *Seiso* ("sweeping and washing"), *Seiketsu* ("good housekeeping"), and *Shitsuke* ("discipline"). Murugan calls the Five S's "simple rules to keep any place clean and orderly, be it your house or workplace."

SELF-MANAGING TEAMS AT TIM

The goal was to have all manufacturing people involved in self-managing work teams by 1993. By June 1992, about 85 percent were members of self-managing teams. Following quality circles, quality at the source, and total productive maintenance/autonomous maintenance, the next important building blocks toward the flexible organization were team daily administration and daily management. Daily administration, explains A. Subramaniam, involves teams' taking on routine activities formerly performed by supervisors: marking attendance, set-up, control of material usage, quality control, monitoring cycle time, safety, and line audits. TIM used several American companies as benchmarks for setting up daily administration for teams. For example, Milliken & Company, which produced textiles, has very good flow and maintains that if a team does good flowcharting, it can reduce problems by 50 percent. Florida Power & Light says that everything they do keeps customer satisfaction in mind, "so each person is challenged to keep the impact on the customer in focus." Japanese companies were also used as benchmarks. Toyota Motor, for example, maintains that employees have to know why certain operations are done the way they are, and so inspired TIM to write down why certain things are done in a certain way. There are written explanations even for marking attendance and housekeeping.

By June 1992, 85 percent of manufacturing employees were members of self-managing teams.

Daily management comes closest to full self-management, as TIM defines it: "A team working together and managing their process without any need for supervision." Mohd Azmi notes that daily management involves "a control activity that incorporates quality, cost, delivery, and service as the customer satisfaction drivers that link all critical sources of problems, from management to the lowest organization level. It involves a standardized procedure for identifying and solving problems and is applicable to every level in the organization." Low Say Sun, training and development administrator, adds, "They are expected in daily management to detect abnormality and take corrective action as well as make improvements in their work area using problem-solving techniques and quality control tools. It will be just like running a business company. Of course there will be facilitators or managers whom they can turn to for help. In other words, there will be somebody to take care of the team. Training will be provided to enable them to manage their operation and process well." To begin, team members receive about 50 hours per person of training in the QC Story, quality control tools for problem solving, team building, daily management, analysis, capacity, communication, and other areas. The training function was increased by eight people, whose sole job is to teach, coach, and support members toward maturity as fully functioning self-managing teams. Many of the trainers are former production supervisors who have been displaced by the changeover to self-managing teams.

DIFFICULTIES ALONG THE PATH

Was everyone equally on board when it became clear that TIM was headed in the direction of self-managing teams? Subra remembered:

"There was concern that some of the senior technicians would not like self-management and want to leave. What we found is that they actually enjoy the teaching aspects and find more fulfillment in doing that than in doing their old jobs.

"The most important thing in this or any program is good communication right from the start. Never hide anything from the workers. Tell them up front what is involved, how long it is going to take, what is their role, how they will be affected. Everything has to be told up front. Our plant manager meets every month, without fail, with all the employees. He has explained during these meetings the basics, and then I follow up with the workers in meetings of thirty people more of the details, answering their questions." [Note that the issue of "senior technicians" is a problem that emerged in other stories in this book.]

Not all managers and supervisors have made the transition. Subra recounts how one manager "completely dominated his team with his self-centeredness. He never was able to adapt to the give-and-take of the team system and the sharing of authority. He wanted to make all the decisions himself." Eventually he left TIM for an electronics company that has a traditional management style. "From a technical viewpoint, we regretted his loss," said Subra. "He was excellent at the technical side, but he was never able to accept the team system. I've talked to him recently, and he's much happier in a traditional management setting."

Some managers and supervisors have not made the transition.

165

Another issue is the question of what to do with former supervisors. This group is quite vulnerable to anxieties, not entirely unfounded, about job security. Many former supervisors have become trainers, facilitators, and technical specialists. Some have chosen to leave TIM. But no one has been laid off.

Did workers ask for more money when they realized self-management meant increased responsibility in their jobs? Subra said they were told up front that there will be no monetary incentive in going into self-management. Even if we were to divide the pay for the supervisory positions that are eliminated among the 1,600 manufacturing employees, it would come to only U.S. $10 per employee. We talk more about the freedom and skill development that they will get." However, TIM is considering a gain-sharing approach. When aggressive improvement goals are exceeded, employees may share the monetary gain.

PERFORMANCE OUTCOMES

One outcome of TIM's quality improvement activities is enthusiastic employees. A technician told Mohd Azmi, "You know, Azmi, before these self-managed teams started, when I set up the equipment and I had problems, I just put a hold tag saying 'hold for engineer' on that lot. The next day, the engineer would come and fix the problem. But you know, now that we have gone through all this training for self-managing teams, and I know why my job is so important in relationship to my customer, I feel very bad. Now I understand. Now I know that if I put the lot on hold for the engineer, I will create one more day of cycle time, which is not good for our customer. Now I know that customer satisfaction is our number one priority."

Low S.S. explains, "Self-managed teams are the way most companies in the future will go. Today's workers are more educated, motivated, responsible, and more capable of doing their job without being closely supervised. We can be proud that TI Malaysia is among the first in TI worldwide to have adopted SMWTS. It is a creative way for you to use your talents and it provides an opportunity to learn and develop yourself to be a better person, while at the same time makes life more interesting and rewarding." Mohd Azmi adds:

"Technicians, in the past, some of them, as they stepped into the plant, parked their brains outside the fence. They came in with a body and hands, and they went to work and they went home. But today, we have got technicians who come to work with a brain and work and also take home work. Can you believe it? And feel happy! I believe it is something the people want, something they really want.

"Teams are the way most companies in the future will go."

Now, by getting into the self-managing teams concept, we are creating an environment where there is a certain amount of freedom to choose what they want to do. I believe some of them who never in the past enjoyed their jobs now have the opportunity to express themselves. And sometimes there are surprises. In the past, we had operators that we assumed were not very smart and couldn't contribute much. Today many of those same people come in and show fishbone diagrams and Pareto diagrams and ask why a certain lot has increased cycle time or why there are other problems. Now they come forward and show us analyses! We are very excited because there is a lot of potential that we can tap if we provide the necessary training, coaching, and support. I think we can get a lot "

As for the numbers,

- TIM attributes a savings of $50 million in 10 years to quality improvements alone.

- There is a significant positive change in attitude, demonstrated by the fact that annual attitude survey results increase each year, and for the last two years, have been among the highest within TI worldwide.

- Thirty-five percent of TIM's production goes to Japanese customers, as opposed to none prior to 1985. Every major Japanese electronics company buys products from TIM, and several have exclaimed that quality at TIM rivals Deming Prize winners in Japan.

- As a result of putting operator self-control into practice, sustainable increases in yield and quality have been recorded. The average outgoing quality part-per-million defect was reduced tenfold between 1982 and 1990.

- In 1989, TIM received Malaysia's Award for Manufacturing Excellence.

- In December 1991, TIM was the winner of the 1991 Ministry of International Trade and Industry Excellence Award for Quality Management.

- From 1980 to 1991, units shipped increased from 400 million to almost 1 billion per year, while the number of semiconductor employees decreased from 2,500 to 2,000, showing a dramatic increase in output per person.

- The operators-to-supervisors ratio increased from 60:1 to 200:1, while the number of supervisor positions decreased from 79 to 18. The plan is to reduce supervisory positions even further.

- There have been demonstrable increases in cleanliness and machine "up time"; the equipment mean time between failures has increased four times and downtime is only 25 percent of what it was in the past.

- Thirty-eight percent of the workers had perfect attendance in 1990.

- Product cycle time has been cut in half.

CONCLUSIONS

As part of its principles, Texas Instruments is committed to achieving customer satisfaction through total quality. Part of the plan to accomplish this end is reflected in the corporate values: "We will create an environment where people are valued as individuals and treated with respect and dignity, fairness and equality. We will strive to create and to achieve their professional goals." TIM takes this philosophy even further with its statement: "Our policy is to foster an atmosphere in which every employee is motivated and capable of using their talent and skill to promote customer satisfaction and customer success." Most

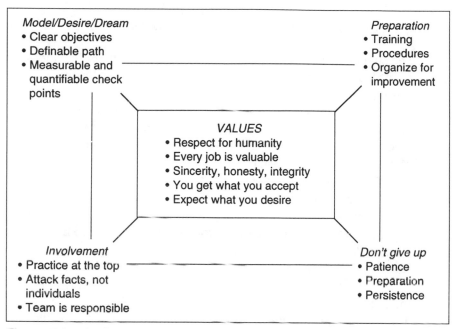

Figure 7.2. Attributes for success.

of all, one frequently hears the word "family" as a metaphor to describe the philosophy and practice at TIM.

Jerry Lee has summarized his concept of the attributes that contribute to the success of TIM (Figure 7.2). The centerpiece of these attributes are the values that relate to the "people" part of the equation. At TIM, total quality management and teams are integrated so that the organization can indeed conduct business without bosses.

Key Lessons for Creating Business Without Bosses

1. The change at TIM has been guided by an overall philosophy that stems first from the parent company, and second, from the unique overlay that TIM uses to interpret this philosophy.
2. The change has been inspired from the top down by an executive, the managing director, who expresses a clear vision that views employee development and self-management as the centerpiece of the drive toward excellence.
3. An evolution of organizational structure from a vertical hierarchy to a flat, delayered form has accompanied the emphasis on self-management.
4. The quest for excellence through total quality has served as the primary driver of the change.
5. Self-managing teams at the production level are a logical extension of the total quality management effort and come only after the principles of quality excellence have been instilled.
6. The organization continues to emphasize training to a remarkable degree; training includes not only technical training but social, organizational, and self-management skill building. Many former supervisors now serve as trainers.
7. The change has been marked by patient but steady progress over a relatively lengthy period of twelve years. At no time was an overnight transformation expected.
8. The change did not take place without some difficulties along the way, since not every employee is at the same level of readiness and capability for adapting to the requirements of the flexible organization.

Chapter 8

The Strategy Team: Teams at the Top

This chapter examines how teamwork at the top can be used for organizational strategy making. The focus is on a network of teams that have emerged throughout the company and how this network interacts to determine and implement business strategy for a growing entrepreneurial organization. For this company, the dominant importance of shared values is a critical element in strategy making. These core values are: to act with integrity, to be fair, to have fun, and to be socially responsible. Strategy is created through a bottom-up process that occurs on an annual cycle. Teamwork is also enhanced through annual executive visits to plants where they "stand in" for a wide variety of employees and through teams at the plant. Most of all, the chapter shows how individual psychological ownership can be a critical element in doing business without bosses.

This chapter was written by Kenneth A. Smith and Henry P. Sims, Jr.

This is a story of how teamwork is used as a critical element in framing and carrying out business strategy. In contrast to previous chapters, this one focuses on a network of teams that have emerged throughout a company because of the commitment of the team at the top—the executive team. Teams and teamwork are an important part of this story, although the company does not routinely use the term "team" in connection with strategy making. Nevertheless, relationships and communication both within and between teams clearly are important parts of strategy making. This bottom-up strategy making is an important element that helps the company to conduct business without bosses.

This company emphasizes the importance of shared values, which both define the company's culture and contribute to the teamlike atmosphere. We have also observed that shared values are major drivers of strategy making in this company.

As we begin, let us clarify what we mean by the phrase "strategy team." In reality, there is no single group at AES to which we might attach this label. Rather, the strategy team is a network of individuals and teams who collectively define strategy.

AES CORPORATION: THE COMPANY

AES Corporation, formerly called Applied Energy Services, Inc., is an independent power producer; it develops, owns, and operates electric power plants and sells electricity to utility companies. All of its current plants are cogeneration facilities, a power generation technology in which two or more useful forms of energy, such as electricity and steam, are created from a single fuel source, such as coal or natural gas.

AES was cofounded as a privately held corporation in 1981 by Roger W. Sant (chairman of the board and chief executive officer) and Dennis W. Bakke (president and chief operating officer). Previously, Sant was assistant administrator of the Federal Energy Administration (FEA) for energy conservation and the environment from 1974 to 1976 and then director of the Energy Productivity Center, an energy research organization affiliated with the Mellon Institute at Carnegie-Mellon University, from 1977 to 1981. Bakke served with Sant as deputy assistant administrator of the FEA and as deputy director of the Energy Productivity Center.

AES was formed in response to certain legislative and business environment changes in the regulated utility industry. In response to the energy crisis of the 1970s, Congress passed the Public Utility Regulatory Policies Act (PURPA). As a result, a significant market for electric power produced by independent power generators developed in the United States. AES was an early entrant to this market and today is one of the largest independent power producers.

AES's stated mission is to help meet the need for electricity by offering a supply of clean, safe, and reliable power. It has pursued this objective by creating a portfolio of independent power plants, all of which use cogeneration technologies. Prior to obtaining financing for its first power plant, most of AES's revenue came from providing consulting services focused on least-cost energy planning for utilities, governmental agencies, and others interested in energy markets. AES still provides these services, although they no longer represent a significant portion of revenues. According to Roger Naill (vice-president), consulting serves as a way to stay on the cutting edge of economic and technological developments.

Since 1983, the company has developed, constructed, and is now operating five plants, with two more facilities under construction, and is pursuing additional projects in the United States and overseas. The combined capacity of the five plants is approximately 860 megawatts of electricity and approximately 400,000 pounds per hour of process steam. The combined total assets of these five plants and related facilities were approximately $1.4 billion at the end of 1991. The two plants under construction have a combined capacity of approximately 430 megawatts and 280,000 pounds per hour of process steam.

Pursuing a strategy of operating excellence, AES has established high standards of operation and has been a leader in environmental matters associated with independent power production. All of the solid-fuel projects it owns and operates employ the very best "clean coal" technologies available, such as scrubbers or circulating fluidized-bed boilers. During 1991, AES facilities' emissions were recorded at levels considerably below those allowed under environmental permits, thereby exceeding the federal performance standards mandated for such plants under the Clean Air Act. AES has also offset carbon dioxide emissions by funding projects, such as the planting of trees in Guatemala and the preservation of forest land in Paraguay.

AES has established a better-than-average safety record for the electricity generating industry. Further, its plants averaged 92 percent "availability" during 1990 and 90 percent during 1991, an above-average measure of plant reliability.

By December 1990, AES was generating $190 million in revenues on approximately $1.12 billion in total assets. It employed approximately 430 people in its plants and at its home office in Arlington, Virginia. In July 1991, it went public, selling approximately 10 percent of the company in an initial public offering. In the same year, the company generated $333 million in revenues on $1.44 billion in assets. By mid-1992, its market value reached $1.7 billion. In October, AES was ranked 58 on *Fortune*'s list of America's 100 fastest-growing companies. Clearly, the market evaluates AES as a substantial success.

CORE VALUES AS A STRATEGIC DRIVER

An important underlying framework for AES's strategy is its four core or "shared" values.

- To act with integrity
- To be fair
- To have fun
- To be socially responsible

These values emerged over time, mainly from the founders and officers, and have now been articulated to the degree that they are written and were published as a part of the prospectus for the initial stock offering of the company. Says Bakke, "The only thing that we hold tightly as to what has to be done are the four values." These values permeate AES and serve to unify the company as it pursues its objectives. They also foster a strong team spirit.

"The only thing we hold tightly are the four core values."

Bakke describes *integrity* as ". . . it fits together as a whole . . . wholeness, completeness." In practice, this means that the things that AES people say and do in all parts of the company should fit together with truth and consistency. "The main thing we do is ask the question, 'What did we commit?' " At AES, the senior representative at any meeting can commit the company, knowing that the team will back him or her up.

Fairness means treating its people, customers, suppliers, stockholders, governments, and the communities in which it operates fairly.

Defining what is fair is often difficult, but the main point is that the company believes it is helpful to question routinely the relative fairness of alternative courses of action. This may mean that AES does not necessarily get the most out of each negotiation or transaction to the detriment of others. Bakke asks the question, "Would I feel as good on the other side of the table as I feel on this side of the table on the outcome of this meeting or this decision with my employee or supervisor or customer?"

Bakke also says, "If it isn't fun, we don't want it. . . . We either want to quit or change something that we're doing." Sant agrees: "It just isn't worth doing unless you're having a great time." Thus, *fun* is the third value. AES wants the people it employs and those with whom the company interacts to have fun in their work. Bakke elaborates: "By fun we don't mean party fun. We're talking about creating an environment where people can use their gifts and skills productively, to help meet a need in society, and thereby enjoy the time spent at AES."

The fourth value is *social responsibility*. "We see ourselves as a citizen of the world," says Bakke. This value presumes that AES has a responsibility to be involved in projects that provide social benefits, such as lower costs to customers, a high degree of safety and reliability, increased employment, and a cleaner environment. "We try to do things that you'd like your neighbor to do."

One might question whether a commitment to these shared values might be detrimental to profits or to the value to the shareholders. "We have specifically said that maximized profit is not our objective," says Bakke. In fact, the company's prospectus stated, "Earning a fair profit is an important result of providing a quality product to [our] customers. However, when a perceived conflict has arisen between these values and profits, the company has tried to adhere to its values—even though doing so might result in diminished profits or foregone opportunities. The company seeks to adhere to these values, not as a means to achieve economic success, but because adherence is a worthwhile goal in and of itself."

"Adherence to these values is a worthwhile goal in and of itself."

How are values at AES connected with strategy? Answering this question deserves careful consideration. Many, if not most, companies define their strategies in terms of profit potential, market share opportunities, or minimization of financial risk. Although these elements are important to AES, the company considers them within a larger framework represented by the question: Does this strategy enhance or diminish our achievements when evaluated within the context of the four shared values? Roger Naill elaborates: "We have a business strategy that has certain goals—for example, the corporate goals in our strategic plan—and our values represent the rules that we play the business game by."

As an example, consider the element of risk. Most corporations seek to contain or minimize the financial risk of a potential strategy, and AES is no exception. For each new cogeneration project, the capitalization and legal entity is deliberately made distinct from the main AES corporation. The project must stand or fall on its own merits without directly threatening the financial integrity of AES as a whole.

Nevertheless, financial risk does not seem to generate the greatest debate and most careful consideration within the company. The issue of whether a potential project (strategy) threatens the shared values seems more prominent. For one project, the company was considering an investor partner for a proposed cogeneration venture. This partner owned a tobacco subsidiary. The so-called risk of this project was not considered predominantly in financial terms but in terms of whether the association with this particular financing partner would be consistent with the shared values of the company. Dennis Bakke provided another example: "When considering what to do about mitigating carbon dioxide emissions and their effect on global warming, the company decided on a strategy of planting and/or preserving trees, including the planting of 52 million trees in Guatemala. This strategic decision turned more on the company's social responsibility value rather than the fact that the cost of tree planting exceeded the company's net profit in the year the decision was made."

Bakke describes the relationship between strategy and values as follows: "There is both a strong linkage and no linkage at all. All strategy for meeting the electricity needs of the world is developed in the context of the shared values. But whether the strategy we choose and implement is successful in actually meeting the world's need for clean, reliable electricity has almost nothing to do with the shared values." Sant elaborates:

> "The thing we made clear was that the values were not likely to change over time. Those were considered fundamental truths. There wasn't ambiguity about them. There might be ambiguity about what's fair or not fair, but there wasn't ambiguity that we really wanted to be fair, and it was not likely to change to wanting to be unfair, whereas strategy is going to change constantly. We may be doing something now that says coal plants are really a great strategy, but we ought to know that those things are going to change. We're not going to get locked into those or, if we do, we're in trouble. So we should be very clear that there are some things that we are tight on. In Bob Waterman's book, *In Search of Excellence*, he called those tight-loose. We're tight, very tight, on values; very loose on almost everything else. What is important, though, is that the strategy chosen not be inconsistent with the values."

"The values are not likely to change over time. They are fundamental truths."

AES's shared values contributed to the team spirit that pervades the company. The content of the values encourages AES personnel to think of themselves not as individuals but rather as members of the AES team. Integrity stresses the need for individuals to fulfill commitments—their own and those made by the company. Fairness generates sensitivity to the positions and perspectives of others, both in and outside the company. Fun, as defined at AES, results from using one's abilities to contribute to the effort of the whole. Social responsibility stresses being aware of and serving the needs of others. Together, these values build an outward-looking orientation in the minds of AES personnel and foster a desire to work with others.

The processes by which the values are implemented and evaluated contribute to AES's team orientation. For example, each manager is rated annually on "values performance"—that is, how he or she performs in relation to the four shared values. According to Bakke, "We rate each other, fifty-fifty, on the basis of technical performance and values performance." More broadly, all AES employees are encouraged to challenge any and all others on how strategic and operating decisions reflect the core values. This fosters an air of mutual accountability and serves as a constant reminder that all are members of the same team. Thus, the shared values contribute to a company-wide culture that is characterized by a teamlike atmosphere. (See the box.)

THE OPERATING COMMITTEE: THE CORE OF THE STRATEGY TEAM

AES's Operating Committee is the core organizational unit through which strategy is developed. Think of the committee as an onion with three layers (Figure 8-1). The inner layer consists of the three founding officers: Sant, Bakke, and Bob Hemphill, the executive vice-president. This is the *core vision team*—the group that provided the initial guiding vision of the company and is still most actively involved in the extension, enhancement, and communication of that vision. This core vision team is also "first among equals." That is, although all members of the Operating Committee have equal access to and opportunity in the strategy process, in practice, Sant, Bakke, and Hemphill are generally seen as having more influence than the others, and typically they are more engaged in managing the core values of the company.

The middle layer of the "onion" consists of company officers who are not founders: Ken Woodcock and Tom Tribone (senior vice-presidents) and Mark Fitzpatrick, Roger Naill, and Barry Sharp (vice-presidents). They have been with AES for several years and carry out important policy and operating roles. This middle layer also has one important external linkage, Roger Naill, charged with leadership of the planning team, which has responsibility for scanning the environment for ideas for new ventures. The planning team also serves as a technology assessment unit that evaluates the potential of new and alternative technologies.

The outer layer of the onion generally contains two groups: the plant managers and the team leaders of new-venture teams. The plant managers carry out the operations of the current energy generating

Executive Plant Visits:
We Have Met "They" and "They" Are Us

An important process through which AES has become a whole unified team has been annual visits of the plants by the corporation's top executives. Dennis Bakke, president:

"Every officer has to go once a year to one plant for a week. Partly symbolic, partly it's a tremendous time to get to know some of the folks. It lets them give us a bad time. They love it, to see us dirty, or whatever—make fools of ourselves. And partly it's a chance for them to tell us what things are right or wrong. While I was out there, I started to realize, 'These people are no different. I don't understand. They have the same motivations, the same concerns, and they like to care about things and about people and about the company. What's different about them? Why are we treating them differently? Why are they being managed in a different way from what we do in Arlington?' I started asking a lot of questions about that. 'Why are we doing it differently? Why are the maintenance people all here in their own group and office people in another? And here are operators, and the operators can't do any of this? Maintenance people have to come and do these kinds of things?' It's the old union thing, where you hold the plug and I'll plug it in. I said, 'Why do we do that?'

One guy was complaining, 'Well, you know, maintenance guys never do this. They never get it done. I put the work order in, and it never gets done. And they wouldn't let us do that. And they . . .' I started saying, 'Well, who in the world is "They"? What do you mean by "They"? 'Well, uh . . . the guys in Arlington,' or 'the people in the administration building,' or 'the plant manager.' They very seldom could tell you who 'they' was, but it was somebody out there. Somebody other than themselves was responsible for their job and making them helpless. We heard all kinds of comments like that. And that bothered us a lot.

Bob Hemphill came up with an idea for a major Anti-They campaign. Everyone had a great time with it. Anti-They. The big international symbol: 'They' with a line through it. Everyone gets caught saying 'they.' Everybody. Even I do. A guy in the control room would say, 'Well, they won't. They don't care. They don't want to do this.' We'd say, 'Who's they?' Now they do it to each other. Trying to get people to say 'we.' In fact, a reporter came out to do a report one time on one of our plants, and that was his headline on the article . . . 'Everybody Says We.' "

The campaign against "they" is but one outgrowth of the annual visitations of senior executives to operating plants. Each executive voluntarily spends at least one week at a specific operating plant—not to review or receive briefings but to participate in the everyday activities of the plant by carrying out the work assigned to a specific job. In essence, each executive takes on at least one job per day, and some of these jobs can be fairly rough or dirty. Bob Hemphill recollects: "Since it was my big idea, I got to go first. It actually turned out that Dennis went the same week I did, in August. We both spent a week doing whatever they told us, basically. And since we had no skills, it meant we got to do whatever was hot, or wet, or dirty, or usually hot *and* wet *and* dirty. And although these are highly automated plants, there's still a bunch of lugging, toting, hauling, lifting and shoving. And it was very, very interesting."

These visits have two positive results. First, it is an opportunity for executives to listen and learn from direct experience on the firing line. More important, it is an extraordinarily vivid symbolic message to each employee. In keeping with the company's core values, it conveys the notion that each job is important, and no one is too good to work at any job—no matter how rough or dirty it is. More recently, company executives have begun a program of reciprocal visits; groups of employees from each location make periodic visits to the company home office at Arlington.

All of these exchanges evoke a strong sense of loyalty, commitment, and sense of ownership throughout the company. In addition to membership in their immediate work team, each employee feels a part of the larger organizational team.

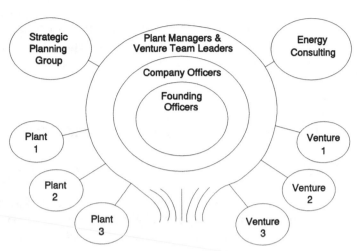

Figure 8.1. Operating committee at AES.

projects. They work at operating locations geographically distant from the home offices in Arlington.

The team leaders are charged with the responsibility of opening and starting up a new project location. These members of the outer layer also serve as important linkages to the other parts of the organization. The plant managers are the primary links to each operating location, and the team leaders are the primary links to the new-venture teams.

Although distinctions between the three layers can be observed in terms of function, the distinctions do not represent rigid separation; the boundary between layers is very porous. The involvement and influence of individuals in the strategy process are largely dependent on personality and interest rather than organizational structure. On some decisions, according to Naill, "A project development leader might be more influential than some officers, just on the basis of their insights and gifts."

Influence on strategy is largely dependent on personality and interest rather than organizational structure.

The Operating Committee serves as the core infrastructure through which the strategy process is carried out. In essence, the committee is a network of teams, of which the core vision team is the most central.

THE STRATEGY-MAKING PROCESS

The strategic management literature distinguishes between the processes of strategy formulation—defining a strategy—and strategy implementation—putting the strategy to work. While this distinction makes theoretical sense, in practice, the line between the two processes is often unclear. This is certainly the case at AES, where issues of formulation and implementation are addressed in an integrated and continuous fashion. In our description, we combine formulation and implementation and call the process strategy making.

Roger Naill states, "We're always changing our strategy. It's changed at least once a year and maybe twice a year every year that I've been here. We never have the same strategy." Indeed, strategic flexibility has been characteristic of AES from the start. In describing the founding of the company, Roger Sant remembers, "We had a whole bunch of notions that were inaccurate. The data were identifying an opportunity of one kind, and the market was identifying an opportunity of another kind. So, as we went along, we adapted to the opportunities and quickly decided that the cogeneration side of the business was the only one worth pursuing."

An Annual Process

AES engages in an annual strategic planning process that is bottom-up in approach (Figure 8.2). The strategic planning group prepares and distributes a book of planning data to all participants in the process. Then one-day strategic planning meetings are held at each plant every September. At these meetings the plant personnel come together to address the strategic direction of their own plant and the company as a whole over the next five years. These one-day meetings are also attended by a senior member of the strategic planning group (Roger Naill or Sheryl Sturges) and, typically, two other officers—one of the core vision team (office of the CEO: Sant, Bakke, Hemphill) and one of the other vice-presidents.

One-day strategic planning meetings are held at each plant every year.

The meeting is led by the plant manager. The agenda is somewhat structured but discussion fairly loose, designed to get people to talk openly about their ideas and their responses to the discussion materials. The corporate officers serve as resources, share information (sometimes through presentations on issues), and carry the results of the meeting back to the home office. Summaries of each meeting are prepared and distributed to members of the Operating Committee.

For the purpose of strategic planning, the corporate home office is treated as a plant. Participants there include the corporate officers and the team leaders of the new-venture groups. The meeting is structured

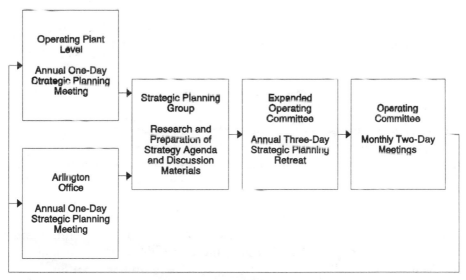

Figure 8.2. AES's strategy-making process.

similarly to the plant meetings, but it provides a forum for addressing the unique needs and concerns of the new-venture teams rather than those of plant operations.

The one-day meetings are, in effect, mini-strategy meetings for the plants. Although corporate strategy is discussed, most decisions at this level are focused on plant- or site-specific issues.

Later in September, all senior management (officers, plant managers, heads of new-venture teams), plus a number of additional representatives from across the company (sometimes chosen at random), meet at a Washington-area retreat center. Attendees at the three-day session, the primary corporate strategy vehicle, are provided with a briefing document (about 200 pages) containing the current strategy statement and reviewing the current market situation, competitors, technologies, and potential customers. This briefing document serves as a basis for brainstorming important issues and decisions facing the company—for example, Should we go public? Should supervisors be elected? Can and should we create a partnership with our plant construction supplier? How should we open our plants? Why aren't we signing more contracts? What changes should we make?

All of the attendees will have attended one or more of the one-day plant meetings, and all have responsibility for initiating issues raised and reflecting opinions voiced at these earlier sessions. As in the one-day sessions, a summary document is prepared and distributed.

A Continuous Process

Strategy making does not end with these annual meetings; rather, the process is much more fluid than the previous description implies. Strategic issues are often dealt with outside the annual planning structure, in a process that is virtually continuous. According to Roger Naill, "We start dealing with issues outside of this structure, as well as in it. What we end up talking about in September ends up sort of being whatever's current in September. Something else will come up in December and we'll deal with that one, and something else will come up in January or March, and we'll deal with that one. We're always changing our strategy."

Strategy making is much more fluid, often dealt with outside the annual planning structure.

By "always changing our strategy," Naill means in an incremental fashion: "You don't really change 'strategies' every few months. Strategic *issues* arise naturally outside the formal cycle, that could lead to a major change in strategy. It doesn't happen often, and mostly, because so much effort is spent thinking strategically during the annual cycle, *strategy* is changed annually."

Issues raised outside the annual planning structure become topics for discussion and action by the Operating Committee and its various subcomponents. In support of the committee's role in the strategy process, the planning group prepares short, focused reports and briefing documents on selected issues that arise throughout the year. For example, one report contained a market analysis that listed all the utilities in the United States and ranked them according to their attractiveness as potential customers.

The Operating Committee meets for two days each month. On the first day, primary attention is given to implementation issues. The manager of each project, from those in the earliest stages of development to plants in operation, gives a short presentation, bringing before the group issues that require brainstorming or decisions. He or she usually identifies several alternatives for action, including the alternative the manager thinks is most appropriate. The discussion following the presentation is likely to address whether the proposed alternative is in accordance with AES's values, as well as the technical and financial aspects of the specific situation. The final decision remains the manager's, but he or she has the resources of the Operating Committee to draw upon.

On the second day, attention turns to more general management issues. Committee members can place any item on the agenda and are encouraged to raise issues that pertain to the values of the company. Topics for discussion may relate to strategy formulation or implementation. One example of a formulation issue related to the core value of social responsibility was, says Bakke, "Should we continue our project in Poland? We face huge problems of poor environment to work in, currency issues, AES people working there, uncertainty about privatization by the government, etc. However, there is great potential for making a positive contribution to air and society." An example of an implementation issue also related to social responsibility was, "Should we build schools for strapped counties around [a U.S.] plant in lieu of taxes that state law exempts us from?" Because the committee addresses both strategy formulation and implementation issues as they arise, the formulation and implementation processes are truly integrated and continuous.

Integrating the Whole

Various groups within the company play different, though overlapping, roles in the strategy process. The corporate officers and especially the core vision team have primary responsibility for defining the core values of the company.

Roger Naill and the strategic planning group provide a unique contribution to strategy making. They do not directly make strategy but serve as the primary information and analysis source from which strategy emerges. Thus, the function of the strategic planning group is not to provide the strategic plan, but, rather, to provide the information necessary for the company to act as "informed opportunists." Naill looks at the role for the strategic planning process as providing information: "It's not to provide a plan. My role is to provide information to the planners, which turn out to be as broad-based a group as we can get in the company. We're actually trying to involve everybody."

The function of the strategic planning group is not to make strategy but to serve as the information and analysis source from which strategy emerges.

The planning group focuses its attention on many strategic issues. Should we be in the coal business or the gas business? Should we be building coal plants or gas plants? What is the Clean Air Act going to do to our business? If the Clean Air Act Amendment passes, should we build fluidized-bed coal plants, or should we build standard boilers with scrubbers? What kind of technology should we be involved in? Analyses of these and other issues result in the briefing documents prepared by the planning group for the annual and monthly meetings.

Members of the new-venture teams, especially the team leaders, also have a unique influence on the direction of the company, sometimes through their own interests and personal objectives. AES is committed to the development of its high-caliber personnel and encourages accomplished new-venture developers to seek out and define their own opportunities. AES became involved in international activities primarily as the result of the interests of several experienced new-venture developers seeking more responsibility and broader opportunities.

Everyone is expected to contribute beyond their primary role.

Finally, plant personnel, especially the plant managers, contribute to the strategy process as it more closely relates to the core business: the cogeneration of electricity and steam. Input from the plants precipitated the strategic concern with operating excellence and continues to define and refine this concept through implementation.

Despite the expected contributions made by each of these groups to strategic management, it is clear that AES expects all participants in the process to be concerned about and take ownership and responsibility for all aspects of the company. Plant managers are encouraged to challenge corporate officers on issues relating to values, new-venture team leaders are expected to provide market information, and the planning group contributes to discussions of operating efficiency.

THE TEAM STRUCTURE

The term "team" is not widely used in everyday vocabulary at AES. Nevertheless, a sense of "teamness" pervades the company. Roger Naill articulated it best: "I don't think 'team' is an AES word, in the sense that we don't go around calling ourselves teams. But the concept is clear. For example, Project Honeycomb [see the box] is very clearly a team-oriented exercise. Work teams at the plant call themselves 'families'. Our strategic planning group is a 'group.' "

The essence of teams is synergy; that is, what is accomplished by

Teams at the Plants:
Operation Honeycomb

AES attempts to evoke employee psychological ownership through the use of teams at the generating plants. As outsiders, we would call these structures "self-managing teams" or "employee involvement teams," but AES uses the term "Honeycomb." Dennis Bakke describes the evolution of Operation Honeycomb:

"Our plants were running wonderfully when we said, 'This isn't really consistent with our values and the way we want people to operate and relate to each other. We need to make huge changes in the way we do operations if we're going to be consistent with our values.' We did this massive change that came to be known as Operation Honeycomb. We changed how our plants are organized and how people relate to each other. It's based on the premise that people will take responsibility and can be trusted. We didn't want arbitrary rules, detailed procedures manuals and handbooks, punch clocks, etc. We wanted a "learning organization," where people close to the action were constantly creating and recreating and where these people were making the decisions—strategy, financial, and capital allocations. For example, I went down and asked, 'What if you didn't have shift supervisors? What if you didn't have this manual that tells you everything to do?' Two months later, they totally revolutionized the place. We discovered these people are no different from the managers. They have the same motivations, the same concerns, and they like to care about people and about the company. Why were we treating them differently? Why were they being managed in a different way?

We outlined several elementary principles to be used in a Honeycomb structure. Cut the number of supervisor levels to improve communication, and get out of people's way. And then one of the plant people came up with, 'Why don't we just divide up into teams?' The next thing I knew, the plant manager called me and said, 'We got this all done. We've implemented it.' They said, 'We're going to call this stuff "Honeycomb," ' and they had worked out all this symbolism regarding beehives and how all the bees were working together.

Of course, the supervisors had to change. Some have adapted extremely well and are real stars. Others moved to special jobs that don't require them to supervise. A few have had to leave completely. So, it's all over the map.

Now, the plants do their own capital allocations. The plant managers decided to change the order of criteria for hiring. First, how well does this person fit with our shared values; then, technical skill. They make almost every decision. They have the responsibility and authority to make every single decision in that plant. There are no exceptions that I know of."

Today, all AES generating plants are organized according to some form of self-managing teams. Since the process of change essentially is implemented bottom-up (although mandated top-down), the specific forms, labels, and language vary considerably from plant to plant. Further, the path leading to self-management has been quite different among the plants. Some were "changeover" of existing nonunion plants; one was a changeover of a union plant; finally, others have been implemented from the beginning.

This variety of implementation and form has given AES a tremendous diversity of experience while adapting to the specific condition unique to each plant. Nevertheless, the conversion to "honeycomb"-like teams has always been inspired and guided by the core values of the organization and always features a bottom-up process that displays great confidence that the employees have a special capability to work out the details of implementation that will suit them best.

Today, the Honeycomb principle is an important part of AES's strategic philosophy. The company believes that operating excellence is a distinctive competence that provides a special competitive advantage. In turn, a critical factor in achieving operating excellence is the responsibility, pride, and sense of ownership that stems from the Honeycomb operating philosophy. "Most important," says Bakke, "is that Honeycomb provides an environment where the 'fun' value can best work itself out for each AES person."

the team is more than could be accomplished by a collection of individuals. By way of analogy, the best basketball teams are those whose members work well together to achieve a common objective. Although individual skills are important, it is their refined combination that maximizes performance. That is why the All-Star games, in which the teams are composed of highly skilled individuals who are not used to playing together, are less elegant than championship games. All-Star teams typically lack the capacity to come together into the well-oiled machines we often see in championship teams.

A sense of "teamness" pervades the company.

For synergy to be achieved, a combination of specialization, interchangeability, and trust is required. Individual team members can contribute to the team effort if they can develop some level of unique skills, but specialization is complemented by a basic understanding and skill level in all of the functions of the team. Thus, to use the basketball analogy again, play makers can take open shots, shooters can rebound, and rebounders can initiate plays. To make the rapid and continuous switching between specialization and generalization within the context of a fast and competitive game, each player needs to be able to trust that teammates can and will make the right play at the right time. Trust provides the confidence to extend oneself to the limit.

Given this definition of a team, AES obviously exhibits team characteristics in numerous ways and at many levels.

The core vision team, each energy-generating plant, the new-venture groups, the strategic planning group, and the Operating Committee all act like teams. They provide a unique stimulus to enhance the motivation, initiative, and self-responsibility of employees throughout the company. Indeed, the word "ownership" best describes how teams influence the psychological perspective of employees. Employees feel ownership in the company and, especially, in their own jobs. Ownership leads to strong motivation and sometimes exceptional effort to perform well (see the box). Thus, individual ownership contributes to organizational competitiveness.

Individual Ownership:
A Team Member Takes Initiative

One of the results of AES's team structure has been a high level of psychological ownership of the company on the part of workers at every level. Such ownership has been an objective of the core vision team since the company's inception. From the beginning, says Sant, the core vision team wanted "something that really makes people feel that they own us. Our instincts were that everybody likes to feel important. *We* did. We'd been in jobs where we were constantly told that we probably weren't important, and we thought that probably wasn't the way to turn young people on."

AES has been extremely successful in attaining the goal of ownership. Dennis Bakke provides this powerful example:

"Let me give you one example of what happened, the kind of thing I think we've had example after example of. We had a guy who, after this Honeycomb process, went Saturday shopping with his wife at one of the discount stores. He was waiting around, waiting for her to get done, and he noticed that they had fans on sale. He looked at the fans, and he realized that they were almost the same kind of fans that we were using at the plant in the process of making gypsum at the back end of our plant. We use a lot of them; they end up wearing out because there's a pretty dirty atmosphere, and so they burn out real fast. He looked and saw that they were selling them for something like $24 apiece, and he remembered that we were spending $75 from the original manufacturer who supplied them at first, and we kept going back to the same guy, at $75. Once or twice a month, we were paying to get new fans. So he immediately took his credit card and bought the entire stock in the store, period. Just bought it.

Now that is the kind of action we're talking about. This is a nonsupervisor, just a regular guy in the plant. What had to be the situation for him? First of all, he had to understand what the

191

technology was, that it was the same kind. He was aware that this was the same kind of fan, or very similar to it, and it would do the same thing in the plant. Second, he had to know all the cost numbers. Third, he had to know that he had authority to do it, that it was safe. And if he was wrong, it would be okay. If he really feared for his job in doing this or that he would have to pay for these hundreds of dollars of fans he had just bought, for a normal guy . . . he knew he would be backed up on it.

That is the epitome of Honeycomb. That responsibility taking. We've had guys who have done that and been wrong. A guy did a whole bundle on an air heater and got it all done, and it was totally wrong—spent, I don't know, $10,000. But no one went back and said, 'That's terrible, and you're getting your salary docked.' We want to encourage that kind of thing. But that's the epitome of the Honeycomb story. We're trying to publicize it and be happy to have more people do it, every day. That kind of wraps it up."

In addition, the use of teams leads to a highly adaptive, nonrigid organizational structure. Job assignments and roles are not engraved in granite, and they sometimes change significantly as the situation demands. The phrase "that's not my job" would be highly incompatible with the team system at AES.

Contrary to most other companies, AES deliberately avoids drawing and publishing a formal organization chart. The use of teams provides an adaptive structure that can change quickly to meet the demands of an emerging situation or a shift in strategic implementation.

Teamwork provides a unique stimulus to enhance the motivation, initiative, and self-responsibility of employees throughout the company.

The team structure strengthens AES's ability to scan its environment and identify strategic opportunities very early. Although the strategic planning group is specifically charged with environmental scanning activities, the new-venture teams—with their external contacts in the market, financial, and regulatory communities—and the plant personnel—with their expertise in operating plants—also provide insight into environmental opportunities and threats.

Teams also contribute to strategic flexibility. Rapid communication among and between teams provides a process for revising strategic implementation without undertaking a whole new formal planning process. In fact, the annual strategic planning cycle is seen mainly as a starting place; often, significant strategic changes are undertaken with short notice.

Before-tax return on investment averaged 46 percent over 1990 and 1991.

Finally, teams contribute to high productivity and competitiveness. Bottom-line results speak for themselves. AES's energy-generating plants significantly exceed industry standards of availability—that is, the proportion of time that energy generation is on line. AES plants typically operate at less than 50 percent of allowable emissions. Voluntary turnover of people is under 1 percent. Accident rates, especially severe accidents, run far below the industry average, and the real cost per kilowatt-hour of electricity produced has been falling for three years. Finally, the company as a whole has maintained high profitability over the years. Before-tax return on sales was 10 percent in 1990 and 16 percent in 1991. Before-tax return on investment averaged 46 percent over the same two-year period.

"We think it's too early to draw long-term conclusions concerning our 'experiment' with regard to these traditional measures of excellence," Bakke is quick to point out. "We are fairly bullish, however, regarding adherence to the values, especially the fun environment that has been created by the decentralized teams and other aspects of the corporate approach."

SUMMARY: A NETWORK OF TEAMS AS THE STRATEGY TEAM

We found the interlocking dynamics between the de facto teams and strategy making at AES unique and provocative. First, strategy making is consistent with a clearly articulated and differentiated set of core values. The philosophy represented by these core values is pervasive and affects strategy making in a profound way. Second, we found that teams were not only useful for the day-to-day issues and operations, as typically found in other companies, but were an essential element in the total strategy-making process. Both within-team and between-team elements provide the crucial structure and process for essential communication that makes broadly based strategy making at AES possible.

Strategy making essentially begins as a bottom-up process. However, the between-team processes, as represented by the annual strategy meeting and the monthly Operating Committee meetings, are the mechanisms that foster aggregation and integration from the diverse parts of the company. Moreover, the bottom-up approach to strategy making provides the means by which the integration of goals, objectives, and ways to achieve them, across all parts of the company, becomes possible.

We suspect that Lawler would call AES a "high involvement" organization, and Manz and Sims would certainly classify AES as a Super-Leadership type of culture.[1] AES emphasizes the importance of teams and teamwork throughout the entire organization. Its executives certainly do not see themselves as bosses, and they clearly have attempted to design a total organization that represents the essence of business without bosses. Whatever the label, AES has found a way to make teamwork an essential ingredient of strategy making through a network of teams. They have defined an exceedingly sophisticated form of the strategy team.

Key Lessons for Creating Business Without Bosses

1. Teams at the top can be driven by a set of core values that pervade the total organization. At AES, these core values are to act with integrity, to be fair, to have fun, and to be socially responsible.
2. Organizational strategies may change in response to a changing environment or new opportunities. In contrast, core values are meant to be enduring, changing little over a longer period of time.
3. Strategy can be formulated and enacted by a bottom-up process that involves the entire organization. At AES, this process flows according to an annual cycle. The key ingredient is a network of interlocking teams, each feeding the strategy-making process.
4. Teamwork is enhanced by intentional contact between top executives and employees at all levels. This contact is expressed by a program of annual executive visits to plants, where top executives "stand in" for employees in a wide variety of jobs throughout the plant.
5. Teams at the top become a model for teams throughout the organization. Teams are not for professional employees alone. Teamwork is apparent at AES from the executive offices to the shop floor.

Chapter 9

Business Without Bosses
Through Teams:
What Have We Learned?
Where Are We Going?

We have completed our journey through several organizations pursuing business without bosses. Now it's time to reflect on the lessons we've learned. How can we best tap the potential of teams for competitive advantage? How can we use teams to improve quality of life for employees and to improve the bottom line? In this chapter, we review the major lessons from the successes and challenges experienced by the teams in this book. We summarize and integrate these lessons in a road map for success.

To some, the notion of business without bosses, is paradoxical and even unnerving. Many organizations, however, have already adopted the use of teams, and by the end of the decade, as many as half of us may be employed in some type of empowered work team environment.

Companies report bottom-line productivity improvements in excess of 50 percent.

Self-managing teams are not just for a select group of people working in unique environments. Teams are employed in a variety of workplaces and by a diverse set of companies. They face difficulties and challenges, but the payoffs are high.

In this chapter we provide a summary of the combined insights that have emerged from the stories in this book. We examine the issues and challenges raised by these stories and suggest some practical prescriptions as organizations consider the introduction of empowered teams. These prescriptions will help us to develop an overall framework—a sort of road map—for the successful implementation of self-managing teams.

PAYOFFS FROM USING SELF-MANAGING TEAMS

Well-implemented self-managing teams have produced some clear benefits. From an organizational point of view, costs frequently go down and productivity goes up. When employees experience greater ownership of their jobs and their outputs, they become motivated and committed. Conflict is reduced. We saw workers describe their operation as "our business" and heard them cheer and congratulate one another when company performance reports indicated positive results for their operation. We observed the significant pride on their faces as they detailed to us the kinds of important decisions they had made and the problems they had solved. They described with obvious pleasure how they saw themselves as important contributors to the organization's performance and progress. Our research shows that these kinds of feelings generally translate into bottom-line financial and output payoffs. Companies have reported dramatic bottom-line payoffs such as reduced manufacturing costs as high as 50 percent and productivity improvements in excess of 50 percent.[1]

The creation of these empowered employee systems resulted in significant advantages for employees too. They experience a higher quality of life at work. Team members told of how they could never go back to the old way of top-down management. They talked about thinking of new work improvements when they were away from work. We saw dramatic examples, such as the employee who stopped by the plant one weekend to make sure everything was okay with his equipment. They clearly revealed an appreciation and pride that put a bounce in their step and look of confidence on their faces.

Perhaps one of the best indicators of this sense of satisfaction was the decreased absenteeism and turnover frequently reported by these organizations. One manager was able to count on the fingers of one hand the number of people who had left his nearly 300-employee self-managing team plant in the last few years. We also saw workers skillfully handle tardiness and absenteeism problems with members of their own group.

Other payoffs could be found in terms of improved quality and increased innovation, which frequently went hand in hand. As employees gained psychological ownership, they took personal pride in the quality of their products and services and worked diligently to eliminate defects and mistakes. In most cases, team members monitored their own output quality. If they detected a quality problem, they initiated action to correct it. Team members also frequently developed creative work procedures to improve quality, efficiency, and service. When work teams combined the experience and knowledge of their various members, they frequently identified innovative solutions to stubborn problems.

Workers take personal pride in the quality of their products and services.

Teams also provided effective mechanisms for resolving employee interpersonal conflicts that might otherwise interfere with performance. Team meetings served as a forum where differences of opinion and hard feelings could be worked out between team members. Effectively integrated teams, which were able to allocate their members more flexibly to address current needs, helped the organization to be more adaptable.

These positive benefits were not realized without cost. Self-managing teams are not a panacea for contemporary organizations. On the contrary, they introduce new problems and challenges. The lessons learned to address these suggest some important prescriptions for achieving success with teams.

CHALLENGES FOR SUCCESSFUL IMPLEMENTATION

A great deal more has been written about the benefits and advantages of teams than about the problems and challenges they raise, especially during the implementation phase. An employee in one company commented that outsiders "seem to think we don't have any problems anymore since we went to teams." Then he went on to describe in some detail the difficult daily struggles teams face. Typically teams face the following challenges:

Organizations tend to expect too much, too soon. Perhaps the notion of teams is now achieving fad status, when managers expect easy implementation and immediate results. To put it another way managers sometimes expect too much, too soon. Recall the original expectation of IDS: executives expected that the design for team implementation would take three and a half months. In fact, the design actually took eight and a half months. Fortunately, IDS management had the patience and the staying power to absorb the frustration of this extended planning period. Their patience paid off with a very successful start-up. Managers who severely underestimate the effort necessary to launch teams successfully are setting up their organizations for failure.

Perhaps the notion of teams is now achieving fad status.

Things often get worse before they get better. Like any other innovation, teams undergo a learning curve. In fact, sometimes organizations suffer a reduction in effectiveness as teams start up, and it may take a year simply to regain former levels. Significant increases in productivity may not become evident for almost 18 months.

This decrease in productivity may occur as team members learn new behaviors and new responsibilities and, especially, struggle to find the path for internal organization that works for them. Many employees have no practical experience with self-management strategies, such as self goal setting, self-feedback, and designing their own information system, so they must learn how to go about these tasks.

Others believe this temporary drop in productivity can be eliminated, or at least reduced, through an appropriate lead time for planning the changeover to teams and intensive training to help team members learn to adjust to and succeed with the new system.

Productivity may initially decrease. Others believe this temporary falloff can be eliminated or reduced.

Finally, management should be aware that employees sometimes test the system to see if management truly has moved to a self-management philosophy. That is, they may deliberately make decisions that they know are contrary to management preferences and then wait to see if management steps in and revokes the decision-making authority. This is a critical moment in any team implementation, because the naysayers, opposed to teams, will be saying, "I told you so!" and management begins to feel as if total organizational effectiveness is threatened. Yet if they step in and overturn a team decision, they will cause a setback that may last for years. The team system itself may fail at this point.

Our experience is that teams do go through a period where they test management but rapidly move on to a higher level of trust and sense of responsibility. Once through this period, they are confident of management commitment and support, they take on some of the challenges of improving quality and productivity that make a real difference to the bottom line.

Managers' and supervisors' sense of power and control is threatened. Frequently, the middle managers and the supervisors feel as if they are the big losers in a transition to team systems. In one sense, they are right; the number of managers and supervisors is typically reduced with a team system. In fact, one of the major sources of savings that derives from a team system is a delayering of management and supervisors.

When an organization changes to teams, managers and supervisors must be guaranteed that none will lose their job because of the new system. (However, they may not be doing the same job or performing the same duties. Also, the commitment does not typically cover job loss due to declining economic factors.) Typically, managers or supervisors who are displaced are reassigned to more technical specialized positions or will be covered over a longer period of time through normal attrition. Recall that the Texas Instruments plant in Malaysia

201

reassigned many former supervisors to training responsibilities. The important point, however, is that management needs to make an up-front guarantee to managers and supervisors that no one will be out of a job because of the team system.

Middle managers and supervisors feel as if they are the big losers.

A more insidious and difficult challenge is dealing with the psychological loss of control that supervisors and middle managers sometimes experience. They have grown up under a system in which the manager is a boss who gives orders, and employees carry out those orders. Typically, they have risen to this position after following orders; now they have the satisfaction of giving orders. They find satisfaction through the power they exercise as the boss.

Most of all, these individuals do not know how to behave in a team system. How can they "get" others to carry out their work if it's no longer legitimate to give orders and instructions—if they can no longer discipline? All of a sudden, their world has turned upside down, and they are indeed frustrated and confused.

These individuals could pose a threat to the team system if they do not allow a team to become self-managing. Perhaps they reverse team decisions if they feel a mistake has been made or if they believe that team decisions are too self-serving, or they may set out to sabotage a team launch, searching for team mistakes and errors and pouncing on these as definitive evidence that "this team stuff will never work!"

Can traditional supervisors be converted to team facilitators or coordinators? Clearly, this change requires both new attitudes and new behaviors, and many are incapable or unwilling to learn these new behaviors. Our experience is that the capability to make this transition is difficult to predict. We have seen the traditional bull of the woods become the most ardent supporter of the team concept. Others are unable to make the transition and must be moved to more technical or specialized functions. Some may retire or quit rather than accommodate themselves to a team system. In a few cases, top management has asked a supervisor or manager who cannot adjust to leave the organization.

Can traditional supervisors be converted to facilitators and coordinators?

Clearly, middle managers and supervisors cannot be ignored when launching a team system; they have the power and the capacity to retard the transition or cause it to fail. They must become part of the solution, not part of the problem, through training and orientation. Sometimes training is almost exclusively focused on the teams themselves, and supervisors are left out. Supervisors and managers must be involved early with orientation, information sharing, and question-and-answer sessions. Mainly, they want to know how they will fit into the new system.

Managers and executives who plan and undertake a transition to teams should prepare themselves for the inevitable: Despite all the training and orientation, supervisors will experience anxiety. Their appetite for reassurance and support—some might call it hand holding—is insatiable. Their psychological disturbance is a part of the change and must be patiently endured and dealt with.

A new perspective on leadership is needed. Occasionally, we see organizations that move to teams but leave untouched the system of managing. That is, we bring in teams to supposedly increase productivity, but the mode of leadership at the management level remains top-down as it always has. Several years ago, one of us met informally with the CEO of a Fortune 100 company that had considerable experience with teams at selected sites within this huge organization yet was unaware of the progress his own company had made with team applications. Perhaps his lack of support is a key indicator of why this corporation has had difficulty diffusing the team concept throughout the whole organization

---

Teams are brought in, but the mode of leadership at the management level often remains top-down.

The automobile industry has been especially troubled by this problem. Ford and General Motors have made considerable progress with teams and employee involvement systems, yet the mode of leadership in the middle ranks of the companies has remained virtually unchanged since the

1960s. Frequently new plant managers with traditional top-down leadership philosophies are assigned to plants with a team system in place.

Decision making tends to be top-down, and highly politicized. GM and Ford have had considerable success with teams. Now the question is, how can they extrapolate this concept to higher levels of the corporation? There is a vast difference in the mode of leadership between such companies as Ford and General Motors, on the one hand, versus AES (Chapter 8) or W. L. Gore (Chapter 6) on the other. We suspect that if every division manager at Ford and GM could take a tour of duty with AES, the competitiveness challenge would be resolved.

Trouble inevitably emerges when a company launches a team system designed exclusively for the lower levels of the organization. At some level in the hierarchy, a large contrast between the way things are done "above" versus "below" will be painfully evident, and somewhere, a manager in the middle will be trying to lead a cluster of teams according to principles of self-management while receiving orders from above in a traditional manner—a troublesome situation posing a severe philosophical conflict. Only an exceptional person can survive under these diametrically opposed expectations.

In a transition to lower-level teams, higher-level management must reexamine its own leadership and teamwork.

Sometimes a change to teams at the lowest level will become a driving force to change the pattern of leadership at higher levels, but this is the hard way to do it. Instead, in parallel to a transition to lower-level teams, higher-level management should reexamine its own leadership and teamwork practices. In essence, the leadership philosophy at the top must be consistent with the team and leadership philosophy represented at the lower levels.[2]

Some high-status employees initially feel like losers. Just like supervisors, some other employees also feel like losers. From our experience, we can generalize some characteristics of employees who are likely to have negative feelings about the change. Employees who enjoy some privilege because of seniority may feel the loss of that privilege. Teams tend to reward and value people more on the basis of performance and contribution rather than seniority. Employees who have achieved a special position, such as specializing in a job with a degree of prominence that derives from a particular knowledge or experience, are more likely to feel a loss. We are reminded of the special clerks at IDS (Chapter 4) who felt resentful because virtually every team member would be trained in *their* expertise. Their niche based on expertise was no longer going to be special. Also, the "techs" in the paper mill start-up (Chapter 3) wanted to maintain their special status, and therefore resented the team system.

Employees who have special knowledge or expertise are more likely to feel a loss.

Managers who are about to embark on a transition to teams should not assume that every employee or category of employee will embrace the team concept enthusiastically. In the planning stage, it may be advisable to conduct an analysis that attempts to identify whether some employees have special stakes in the existing system that they are reluctant to part with.

These employees can be dealt with in several ways. Bluntly forcing the change upon them will cause resentment. Sometimes these employees leave the system, and sometimes they cause distress to the team implementation. A better approach is to involve them in the transition planning process and attempt to deal with their concerns. Sometimes their special status or pay might be grandfathered into the new system. Most of all, it's important for management to realize that not all employees will see a transition to teams as a winning proposition, and these employees can cause considerable damage to the transition.

Employees need expanded technical and behavioral skills. Added responsibility and expanded autonomy means that both the technical and behavioral skill repertoire of employees must be expanded. One of the fundamental changes typically accompanying a team implementation is the notion that a team member becomes capable of most, if not all, of the tasks required of a team. Typically, task or technical-oriented training is required to ensure that team members develop these skills.

But perhaps more important, and not as well understood, is the idea that team members must develop individual and group self-leadership capabilities. They need to learn organizational, planning, interpersonal, and self-direction skills. For example, they must learn how to set goals, interpret feedback systems, lead and participate in meetings, resolve conflicts, and initiate problem solving on their own rather than automatically shifting the burden to a supervisor.

Team members must develop their individual and group self-leadership capabilities.

Team implementation requires planning and organization. Recently, we have heard of organizations that have formed teams by removing the supervisor and making a grand pronouncement that from henceforth the work groups are teams. This approach—with no training, no design, no organizational change strategy—is a sure recipe for failure. The general logic behind this implementation strategy is that teams that are really self-managing will also be able to self-manage the implementation. The flaw in this logic is provided by the rubber band metaphor. A rubber band can absorb a limited amount of stress by stretching; however, if it is pulled too much, too soon, it breaks. Self-managing teams can also break.

Typically, failure comes because teams are given total responsibility without the necessary technical and social knowledge and skills. Teams need to be trained in the fundamental social processes of learning to lead a meeting, to generate creativity, to conduct a problem-solving session, to engage in conflict resolution, and, most of all, to develop leadership skills.[3]

Too much, too soon, and the rubber band breaks. Self-managing teams can also break.

A total quality management approach needs integration with a self-managing system. A wave of total quality management (TQM) is currently sweeping the country. Often, a TQM program is implemented mainly as a technical innovation, and the critical social skills are ignored. Many TQM programs try to place a quality overlay on an existing traditional management/leadership system, with no real fundamental change to the hierarchical approach. Yet to take total quality management to its logical end, a team system is necessary. Moreover, the team system cannot be partial or voluntary or superimposed on a traditional top-down type of leadership philosophy. A fundamental change is needed. If TQM does not include real changes to the fundamental way of doing business, then the prospects for failure are high. On the other hand, if TQM is integrated with a true self-managing system, the two can work hand-in-hand to move the organization to competitiveness.

Many TQM programs are an overlay on an existing traditional leadership system.

"Greenfield" sites are easier than "retrofit" changes. By "greenfield," we mean a start-up situation, where the team system is tightly integrated into the organizational structure from the very beginning. A "retrofit" (or "brownfield") means an organizational change where an existing traditional organization is changed over to a team system.

In a retrofit change, the challenges of implementation are considerably more intense. First, a significant amount of "unlearning" must take place, before the new learning can replace the old. One of the main issues is the behavior of supervisors. Many have years of experience with a particular pattern of leadership—typically top-down. To become a facilitator or coordinator, a supervisor must act in ways that are directly contrary to years of experience—a difficult situation.

In a greenfield situation, the managerial tool of selection is available. That is, the management team can devise tests and selection mechanisms to evaluate an applicant's potential cooperation and team skills. For greenfield sites, this selection perspective is an important part of success. In contrast, in a retrofit implementation, selection is not available. The personnel who staff traditional organizations are the same people who *must* staff the self-management system, and they may not be the most suitably experienced or tempered to succeed in a team system.

This particular challenge is a troubling paradox. Greenfield applications have a higher probability for success, but we suspect that 80 percent of the need for self-managing teams is with existing organizations. Yet it is not feasible, practical, or ethically correct to launch a wave of old-plant closings in favor of new-plant start-ups. The truth is that the vast majority of team applications will be retrofits rather than greenfield applications.

We do not wish to be pessimistic about the potential of changing existing organizations. We have observed many successful retrofit applications, and many of the stories told in this book are retrofits. It's important to accept this reality and then develop and hone the technology of change so that a retrofit to a team system becomes a more certain and routine exercise.

Teams are difficult to diffuse throughout the organization. Several years ago, Richard Walton wrote about the difficulty of diffusing the team concept throughout a total organization.[4] Often, success with teams at one location does not necessarily mean that teams will be implemented at another location. Walton speculated that the team concept might threaten other managers, and it even seemed to be resented by other parts of the organization.

As another example, one of the authors visited a food manufacturing plant that had been extremely successful with teams for more than a dozen years. The plant was a constant contributor to corporate profits, and was also well known for its creativity and innovation. Still, more than a half-dozen other plants in the same company had not yet moved to a team system.

Success with teams at one location does not mean teams will be introduced at other locations.

Perhaps one explanation for this failure to diffuse is the so-called not-invented-here syndrome; that is, "If we didn't invent it, it must not be any good." We personally encountered this attitude at one company, when a manager exclaimed, "If it's any good, then someone else would have done it and written it up!" Unless this manager changes his thinking he is doomed to being an imitator for all of his life.

In addition, we believe that learning about teams is not something that can typically be completely accomplished in the abstract—by reading about teams, for example. Real learning takes place only when teams are experienced. Our own best learning has taken place through hours and weeks of observation of teams. Further, we also experience teams in our own universities, where faculty are typically grouped into areas or departments to accomplish their teaching, service, and research objectives as a team. Executives and managers serious about learning about teams must visit sites with teams and talk to team members. Sometimes these individuals may not be able to write or speak publically about their experience, but quiet conversations about their personal team experience is extraordinarily revealing.

In the long run, we suspect that the diffusion of teams is impeded mainly by the difficulty many managers have in understanding and having the faith that ordinary workers are capable of and willing to undertake the responsibilities that teams require. We continually encounter this perspective in our executive development workshops, although, to be fair, the percentage of executive development participants who are pessimistic about the potential of teams has significantly decreased over the 12 years that we have been doing training in this area. As more and more organizations become successful with teams and as more and more articles about teams appear in *Fortune* and *Business Week*, top management perspectives will continue to change.

LEADERSHIP AND TEAMS

Leadership, a critical element if teams are to be successful, has been a recurring theme throughout the chapters of this book; nevertheless, we wish to state our case one last time.

First, let's reexamine leadership at the first-line level, that is, the supervisor or foreman of so-called traditional work groups. The following behaviors are typical of a person assigned to that role:

Direction	Assigned goals
Instruction	Hierarchical conflict resolution
Command	Reprimand
Assigned jobs/tasks	

There is nothing bad or necessarily ineffective about these behaviors. After all, these are actions we would expect from a foreman, and most of us wouldn't question the legitimacy, the right, or even the effectiveness of such behaviors. But for these behaviors to work, they must take place within a traditional top-down hierarchical system.

In a participatory system, these behaviors are wrong, especially if we want to go all the way with self-managing teams. The ideas of direction, command, and hierarchical conflict resolution are totally inconsistent with a self-management philosophy. If allowed to run freely, these behaviors would destroy a self-managing team. In such a system, a different type of leadership is required, one in which the main focus of the leader is to get the team to lead itself (in our previous book, we call this *SuperLeadership*). The following types of behaviors are necessary for leaders of self-managing teams:

Encourage self-goal setting.

Encourage self-evaluation.

Encourage high self-expectation.

Facilitate self-problem solving.

Develop self-initiative and responsibility.

Encourage within-group conflict resolution.

Provide training.

Encourage opportunity thinking.

Overall, appropriate leadership is a prime ingredient for success with teams. The nature of this leadership needs to change from traditional top-down approaches. Even inspirational visionary leadership, which can foster dependence on the leader, is not a good fit. Leading teams requires an approach that centers on helping teams to lead themselves. In the end, leadership must be spread throughout the organization, especially among team members. SuperLeadership and self-leadership are at the heart of success with teams. Bosses are out; leaders are in.

SOME OVERALL CONCLUSIONS

Our dozen years of conducting research on self-managing teams has given us a certain perspective about teams and their place in the competitiveness challenge. Our conclusions follow.

The fad of quality circles has run its course. Around 1980, about the time we were beginning our research on self-managing teams, quality circles were the rage in U.S. manufacturing. They were a movement in which many U.S. managers and executives discovered that so-called ordinary workers had a capability of contributing something extra, and they provided a transition or bridge from the strictly traditional organizations of the 1950s and 1960s. Nevertheless, unlike self-managing teams, circles were essentially an overlay to the existing organization rather than a true change to the existing way of doing business.[5] Many circles were adopted because they were trendy. And although many quality circles made a contribution, the overall experience was mixed. Most of all, the fundamental way of doing business didn't change.

It seems quite clear that the fad of quality circles has run its course. Many companies are still using circles to some benefit, but the trend is on a decreasing curve. The question has been, What lies beyond quality circles? Is there a next step?

Until the late 1980s, self-managing teams were a well-kept secret. Experimental work with self-managing teams was underway in the United States throughout the 1970s; however, with a few exceptions (e.g., the Topeka Gaines dog food plant), much of the early experimental work was either kept secret or received little attention from the business press. In the early 1980s, it seemed to us that the attention to quality circles was out of balance compared to the more effective self-managing teams. It was almost like teams were a secret, known only to a few insiders.

Finally, knowledge about teams came forward in the late 1980s. Cover stories by *Fortune* and *Business Week* seemed to us to be a milestone. Teams had emerged from the closet to the front pages.[6]

Teams are a deeply rooted organizational change. Perhaps this is the reason self-managing teams received so little attention for almost a decade. Many executives were not philosophically ready to accept the idea that ordinary workers can be trusted to manage their day-to-day activities without someone looking over their shoulders.

Quality circles allow an existing traditional organizational system to continue, with relatively little change to the organizational fabric. In contrast, self-managing teams are a fundamental change in philosophy, attitudes, behavior, and organizational structure. The decision to go to teams is not evolutionary but revolutionary.

Teams are a demanding and challenging implementation. Even when a team implementation is successful, it's not done without considerable patience, dedication, and allocation of resources.

Teams can supply the competitive edge. Despite the difficulties, the real question is whether teams are worth doing. Our answer is a strong yes, provided it's done intelligently and effectively. The evidence is becoming clearer that teams can provide better productivity, higher quality, and a better quality of life for employees. The stories recounted in this book describe organizations with highly satisfied, motivated, and committed employees who have demonstrated unusual initiative and innovative problem solving. These organizations experienced large cost savings and vastly improved quality, with much less absenteeism and turnover in their work force. Overall, major bottom-line benefits were obtained while providing employees a more rewarding environment in which to work. We don't claim that teams are the complete answer to the competitiveness challenge, yet they are a critical element. Any company seeking a competitiveness edge over the next decade should be considering how self-managing teams can facilitate this effort.

Teams enable the working person to participate in life at work in a meaningful, dignified way. Our intention is not to write about teams as "do gooders"; we are not primarily motivated by humanistic ideals. From a management perspective, we think that teams are important because they work. They are effective. Nevertheless, it is important to evaluate how teams typically affect the ordinary person who goes to work every day. Teams are not paradise at work, yet people who work in self-managing teams are generally more satisfied and experience an enhanced quality of life at work. For the most part, people like teams.

The challenge of the decade is to extend teams to knowledge workers. To date, most of our experience comes from the manufacturing sector, yet the team concept is being extended to the service sector, especially so-called knowledge workers. The chapter on IDS is especially instructive in this regard. We suspect that the IDS experience is a forerunner of the most exciting applications of teams into the new century.

We are less optimistic about the government sector, where teams are rare.[7] We see no substantial trend of self-managing teams in the public sector. Perhaps the old stereotype of government bureaucracies that resist change has placed too great a roadblock in the path of any significant progress with teams.

REQUIREMENTS FOR SUCCESS

Certain ingredients will help facilitate the success of self-managing teams.

Self-managing teams must begin with a fundamental philosophy.[8] A fundamental belief in the capacity of humans is necessary. To some degree, this relates to the old Theory Y/Theory X viewpoint. Theory Y describes a set of assumptions that articulates that people will generally respond in a responsible way if given the opportunity and the resources; thus, people are capable of performing creatively and effectively within their repertoire of skills without close external supervision and direction. Theory X, in contrast, assumes that people are inherently lazy and irresponsible and will choose to behave badly if not watched.

We believe that a fundamental philosophy that is optimistic about the capacity of people to respond to opportunity is an important prerequisite for a successful launch of self-managing teams.

Teams will require a change in the management information system of the organization. The increases in employee responsibility and empowerment require a great deal of information for teams to be able to make effective decisions and to perform successfully. In fact, teams will demand information systems and design their own if they need to.

Continuous training is required. The training requirements for teams cannot be overestimated. Moreover, the training must include both technical and task training and sophisticated interpersonal and social training.

Outside facilitation is extremely helpful. This outside help need not come from an expensive consultant. For large companies, an internal facilitator from a staff department or from some other unit may be more appropriate. The main point is that an outside consultant can provide an objective viewpoint that will help to overcome the bumps and challenges that invariably arise.

Finally, we preach patience, patience, and more patience— remember the learning curve. We typically think of a learning curve in regard to the adoption of new technology; yet the development of new social skills that are inherent to self-managing teams also requires a learning curve. Many mistakes will be made; the way is laden with difficulties. Yet think of self-managing teams as an investment. Commit the resources now, and reap the rewards in the future. Patience is the key.

A ROAD MAP TO SUCCESS

Figure 9.1 summarizes some of the primary challenges to success with self-managing teams. More important, it identifies some key steps for avoiding these pitfalls with the final goal of creating effective high-performing businesses without bosses. In a sense the figure presents a basic road map for success.

We have identified dozens of important issues and lessons for self-managing teams throughout this book, and our road map to success highlights some of the most common themes that emerged from our studies. Use this map wisely to help you navigate the challenging but rewarding road to a successful organization in which teams and leaders substitute for bosses. In these organizations, business is done not as usual but with higher performance, quality, and dignity and satisfaction for employees.

A PREAMBLE FOR THE FUTURE OF BUSINESS WITH LEADERS BUT NOT BOSSES

We are face to face with a revolution in the workplace, and many organizations are meeting this challenge head-on. Despite some frustrating problems, organizations that are moving toward business without bosses through teams are experiencing significant payoffs. At the center of these SuperTeam organizations is a shift in leadership thinking and practice.

In the preface to our previous book, *SuperLeadership*, we wrote, "The word 'leader' conjures up visions of a striking figure on a rearing white horse, crying follow me. . . . We think of historical figures . . .

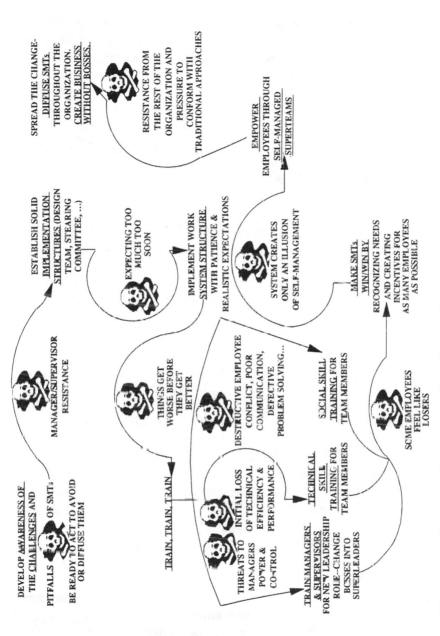

Figure 9.1. Road map to success with self-managing teams.

215

Alexander the Great, Napoleon, George Washington, Churchill. . . . Is this heroic leadership figure the most appropriate image of the leader of today?''[9] We go on to argue the necessity to rethink the essential ingredients of effective leadership.

A number of leadership myths are frequently used as unspoken but commonly held criteria for effective leadership. Leaders are expected to have the answers, to light the way, to know all and see all. In short, they are expected to be bosses who control everything because they are more than human. The reality, of course, is that leaders are human, just like everyone else. Even more important, if the spotlight focuses on the leader too long or too much, a condition of follower dependence and weakness is fostered, and the system becomes limited to the knowledge and abilities of one fallible human being—the boss. When the boss leaves, the system is likely to collapse.[10]

Recent advances in democracy across the globe demand a leadership role from more and more people; they signal a need for greater self-leadership from citizens throughout the world. Dramatic changes in the workplace toward worker empowerment, especially self-managing work teams, are forcing us to rethink what we mean by leadership and how it is performed. These trends call for a movement away from leaders who dominate the spotlight and their followers—away from bosses, away from dependence of the many on the few, and away from wielding power instead of empowering others.

These are the forces that led us to develop our ideas on SuperLeadership—leading others to lead themselves. SuperLeadership is designed to develop others into self-leaders.[11] It is an approach to leadership in which followers become pillars of strength throughout the system. When the leader (*not* a boss) departs, the system is able to continue. Many believe that if things seem to go as well without the leader, he or she was not needed at all. The reality, however, is probably summed up best by the words of the ancient Chinese philosopher Lao-tzu: "The best of all leaders is the one who helps others so that eventually they do not need him."

Teams fit well with the democratic principles of our nation. Interestingly, our major organizations frequently seem to be based more on principles of dictatorship and limiting individual freedom. The term "boss" and what it has come to mean reflects this approach. In the end, however, we seem to be relearning what our forefathers apparently already knew: leadership energy needs to come from within the people themselves. Thomas Jefferson put it well in the Declaration of Independence: "We hold these truths to be self evident, that all men are created equal, that they are endowed by the creator with certain unalienable rights, that among these are life, liberty and the pursuit of happiness . . . that whenever any form of government becomes destructive of these ends, it is the right of the people to alter or abolish it." Years later, in the Gettysburg Address, Abraham Lincoln wrote: "we here highly resolve that these dead shall not have died in vain . . . and that government of the people by the people and for the people shall not perish from the earth."

Creating business without bosses through self-managing teams is the most powerful organizational tool we know for moving us in the direction painted by these inspiring words of our forefathers. Indeed, teams provide a viable way to more fully recognize the value of each person and to achieve elements of a better life, liberty, and even happiness through a work structure characterized by self-governance. The potential benefits for the organization in terms of productivity, quality, and cost savings are compelling. Further, leading others to lead themselves and not bossing them is a perspective on leadership that is consistent with these ideals and holds much promise for helping us through challenging times

We cannot overstate the importance of recognizing that we need one another if we are to recapture our competitive edge and successfully meet the demands of the new century. We need the best that everyone has to offer. Each employee must become a self-leader— a confident, capable, uniquely valuable resource within a business without bosses. Managers and leaders will only be as effective as their followers because employees are the source of strength and wisdom that can help them soar to new heights. Bosses just don't allow this to happen.

Teams not only provide advantages from a humanitarian view and are consistent with lofty ideals, they work. In this book we have told the stories of several very successful organizations that have already learned that if they can replace the excess weight of bosses and harness the power of SuperTeams, they can fly to unforeseen new heights.

THE PATH FOR THE FUTURE: SUPERTEAMS AND SUPERORGANIZATIONS THROUGH BUSINESS WITHOUT BOSSES

A revolution is in progress in the workplace. Many organizations are successfully meeting the competitiveness challenge with a significant shift toward teams. Teams do pay off.

We began this book by elaborating on our title, *Business Without Bosses*. We stated that the old concept of boss was headed to a dinosaur graveyard. But while bosses are out, leaders and teams are in. SuperLeaders and SuperTeams are the wave of the future.

When done right, teams do work!

There is no one recipe that will answer the competitiveness challenge. Yet, through our explorations of teams, we have discovered some important strategies that can help organizations survive and thrive. *Teams are at the center of the competitiveness revolution.*

Fundamentally, business without bosses is good business because competitiveness is enhanced. Teams lead to improved productivity and better quality. They provide a sense of dignity and fulfillment for the working man and woman.

Most of all, teams work. If we can harness the power of Super-Teams, our organizations can fly to new heights. These are the companies that will soar into the twenty-first century. With teams, we really can run a business without bosses.

Appendix

How to Get
What You Want
from Your Job

Is your job less than totally satisfying? Is productivity or quality a problem at your office or plant? Henry P. Sims, Jr., professor of organizational behavior at Pennsylvania State University and a professional engineer, says his studies show that "self-managed work teams" may be the answer for these and other troubles, too.

Q Professor Sims, why do so many people come home from work convinced that they haven't accomplished much?

A They go to work with the idea that they have something to contribute, that their input is important and useful. Frequently, when they get there, they discover that no one really cares about what they think, all that's cared about is whether or not they can carry out a routine task. So people feel underutilized.

Q Is this the way that most companies are run today?

A It's obvious that we have a problem like that with many offices and factories. There *has* been a significant change, though: Twenty-five years ago, a much larger proportion of workers were willing to tolerate those conditions in return for economic security. Today, security is just not enough. Folks are much more demanding in what they want from their jobs.

Q And what they want is—

A Without doubt, almost everybody wants more control over his or her job. Surveys show this.

The surveys also bring forth another interesting point. If you ask supervisors how much autonomy their people have, they will say, "Quite a bit." But if you ask the subordinates, they reply that they have significantly less control over what they do. So there's quite a difference in perceptions. I think that's one of the reasons that satisfaction in jobs has been decreasing in the U.S. in recent years.

Q Do people perform better if they exercise substantial control over their jobs?

A If it is a routine task, the answer may be no. On the other hand, if we're interested in creativity or innovation—and especially if we're interested in what we still think of as pride of craftsmanship or the *quality* of work—then the feeling of control over your own work is very important. Lack of control and a feeling of lack of responsibility over one's work lead to sloppy workmanship, which in turn leads to products of relatively low quality.

Companies without strong foreign competition might be able to get away with that for a lengthy period of time. But, sooner or later, it catches up with them. That's what happened to our automobile industry two or three years ago, and we are just now pulling out of that.

Q How are employers helping their workers become better self-managers?

A That's the $64 question nowadays in American industry. There are many ways, but one I see most often is the "team" concept.

In the traditional plant the foreman assigns jobs, tells workers how to do their work and enforces performance standards, frequently using reprimands. The employee is expected only to carry out a simple task, and it's up to the foreman to resolve problems or to seek technical help.

But in some companies now much of the problem solving and direction is coming from *within* self-managed work teams rather than from a representative of management. Typically, the members of a team have a group of closely related tasks.

Q What's unusual about how these teams work?

A I'll use as an example the work teams that Dr. Charles Manz, my collaborator, and I have observed at a General Motors plant.

A team negotiates within itself to determine who should do particular tasks. The assignments aren't done by a foreman. Sometimes they work out scheduling, too—perhaps come in 4 hours early on Friday in order to leave 4 hours early.

They get substantial feedback from management: How much they're producing, how it compares to the past and to other plants. They talk out their problems. Perhaps someone in the team is not sharing information on how to best do a particular job, and someone else therefore is having troubles.

Q As a result, is there more productivity? Are attitudes improved?

A The products from this particular plant are being produced at a cost that is at least as good, if not better, than anywhere else at GM. It's one of the outstanding performers in terms of cost efficiency and product quality.

The people at this particular plant are given a rather extensive attitude survey each year. In the past, the level of job satisfaction of the ordinary worker in this plant has been higher than that of professional engineers and supervisors at GM.

I've never seen a plant in which people were so deeply involved in what they were doing and aware of the economic consequences. I watched a production worker decide what grade of coal to use for melting scrap metal based on changes in the price of coal.

I saw another hourly worker get up from the line and do his own chemical test in a laboratory when he suspected some materials were not up to specifications. His suspicions were correct, and he saved GM a lot of money. I saw other workers meet together to solve a severe quality problem. They suggested several important changes that were not apparent to management.

People who do things like this have remarkably good attitudes. They feel like they have a lot of autonomy.

Q Isn't the concept of autonomy more easily applied to white-collar than to blue-collar jobs?

A Generally, yes. White-collar work, in a sense, implies a certain amount of discretion and judgment that one brings to the job. But you needn't equate white-collar work with being self-managed, or blue-collar work with not being self-managed, because I've seen many exceptions.

An engineer might be hired to carry out technical details of a project, yet have virtually no decision-making responsibility. So you can still find a tremendous lack of self-management even in white-collar jobs.

Q Don't many managers feel afraid or threatened when subordinates are given more responsibilities?

A Managers, of course, think they're very capable of making decisions. After all, that's part of being a manager. So a manager who wants to develop self-management capabilities in subordinates must encourage them to make decisions.

There's risk involved. Sooner or later, the subordinate will make the wrong decision. But if you're going to develop self-management capability, you'll have to expect a few bad decisions. You have to think of it as an investment: People can learn from their mistakes, but the only way for them to learn is for them to stick their necks out.

I think the major deterrent to the spread of self-management concepts, by the way, is that managers feel like they're losing control of the situation. I certainly detected some of that with the team approach at General Motors. Some people at higher levels sometimes feel uncomfortable when a work group is making decisions that the managers once made. The manager has to have a great deal of self-confidence in terms of being willing to live with the results of whatever the team comes up with.

Q What can people do to sharpen their self-management abilities?

A Charles Manz and I typically suggest several strategies:

First is self-observation. This means observing your own behavior and its consequences. I can give a personal example. Sometimes at meetings I feel that I'm talking too much. It's a typical professorial malady. There are times to talk and times to listen, but it's an effort to control my own behavior.

One way for me to do that is to take a piece of paper and put a check mark every time I have something to say. I can then tell whether I'm saying too much. At the GM plant, each team is provided with substantial feedback about their efficiency, their output, their quality, their safety, etc.

Second, specify your goals—where you want to be or what specific tasks you want to accomplish. Athletes are extraordinarily good at this. Runners typically challenge themselves by shooting for timings that are somewhat challenging but still achievable. Research has shown that achievement-oriented people also are good at setting moderately difficult goals.

One form of goal setting is to keep lists. I do this, and virtually every executive and every effective professional person that I know does, too. Each team at the GM plant participates in goal setting, including an annual budget proposal. Can you imagine blue-collar workers proposing their own budget?

A third strategy is to arrange your work environment in a way that helps you accomplish those goals. If you wish to write and need to concentrate as you write, then find a place that's out of the way and won't let you be distracted. Getting away from the telephone may help, too. For a team at the GM plant, it means making sure they have enough material on hand to meet their goals.

Q Are there other techniques that people can use?

A You can modify your incentives.

Self-reinforcement is relatively effective, and most of us engage in this to some degree—sometimes without recognizing it. A salesman who closes a deal in the afternoon will go back to his motel in the evening and eat a special steak and order a special bottle of wine to celebrate. In essence, he is rewarding himself for the achievement of a goal.

We also have internal rewards—a mental pat on the back where you say to yourself, "I feel good about doing that." When I finish making a speech before a group of executives, for example, the most important reward for me is my own feeling that I've done the job well. For self-managed work teams, reinforcement from each of the members is important.

Self-punishment is the opposite: A feeling of guilt when we fail to do something. Some people are motivated by self-punishment, and especially by fear of failure. But for most people it's just not very effective in the long run.

Finally, you can rehearse—practice your desired performance. A new salesman might practice a sales call with an experienced sales manager. But you also can rehearse mentally— think about what you are going to say and do in a given situation. Research has shown that mental rehearsal helps you perform better later on.

Q These suggestions seem to be aimed at white-collar or independent workers. Do they apply equally to employees involved in production?

A They are quite consistent with the strategies involved in teaching a production team how to be self-managed. Successful people in almost any sort of job are always applying these kinds of strategies right now, whether they explicitly realize it or not.

Q What about the worker whose boss says, "I don't care what you think— I'll make all the decisions"?

A There's no question that the philosophy in an organization has a lot to do with how far you can carry self-management concepts. Everybody under takes self-management to some degree—until they run up against constraints imposed by others.

In my work as a professor, I have very little constraint on how I manage my work. It's in the nature of academic freedom to have a great deal of flexibility to pursue whatever scholarly interest I want.

At the opposite extreme is the man on the assembly line who is given virtually no discretion at all in when or how or why to do his work. But even when technology is relatively constraining—which was the case at the General Motors plant—a creative manager can organize people into teams and give them some responsibility for solving the problems that revolve around their own particular jobs.

Q Can many workers ever expect the chance to manage their own jobs?

A We're starting to see some marvelous successes of this idea in the U.S. I think there's a wave of change occurring in factories right now. In different forms, this concept is under consideration at virtually every large manufacturing corporation, and it's beyond the talking stage. Corporations are now investing significant amounts of time and energy and money to undertake these changes. I'm optimistic!

Endnotes

Introduction

1. *New York Times*, January 18, 1993, p. D4.
2. This section is based in part on Charles C. Manz and Roger Grothe, "Is the Workforce Vanguard to the 21st Century a Quality of Work Life Deficient-Prone Generation?" *Journal of Business Research* 23 (1991): 67–82.
3. See, for example, Joseph A. Raelin, "60's Kids" in the Corporation: More Than Just 'Daydream Believers,' " *Academy of Management Executive* 1 (1987): 21–30.
4. See "Baby Busters Enter the Work Force," in *Futurist* (May–June 1992): 53. The article is based on Lawrence J. Bradford and Claire Raines, with Jo Leda Martin, *Twenty Something: Managing and Motivating Today's New Work Force* (New York: Master Media Limited, 1992).
5. "The New Industrial Relations," *Business Week*, May, 1981, pp. 84–88.
6. From a speech given at the International Conference on Self-Managed Teams, University of North Texas, Denton, Texas, 1990.
7. Brian Dumaine, "Who Needs a Boss?" *Fortune*, May 7, 1990, pp. 52–60.
8. John Horr, "The Payoff from Teamwork," *Business Week*, July 10, 1989, pp. 56–62.
9. This section borrows heavily from Henry P. Sims, Jr., and Peter Lorenzi, *The New Leadership Paradigm* (Newbury Park, Calif.: Sage, 1992).
10. Horr, "The Payoff from Teamwork."
11. Dumaine, "Who Needs a Boss?"
12. Madeline Weiss, "Human Factors: Team Spirit," *CIO* 2 (July 1989): 60–62.
13. Lee W. Frederiksen, Anne W. Riley, and John B. Myers, "Matching Technology and Organizational Structure: A Case in White Collar Productivity Improvement," *Journal of Organizational Behavior Management* 6 (Fall–Winter 1984): 59–80.
14. John B. Miner, *Theories of Organizational Structure and Process* (Hinsdale, Ill.: Dryden, 1982), pp. 110–111.

15. Paul S. Goodman, Rukmini Devadas, and Terri L. Griffith Hughson, "Groups and Productivity: Analyzing the Effectiveness of Self-Managing Teams," in *Productivity in Organizations* (San Francisco: Jossey-Bass, 1988).
16. Barry M. Macy, Paul D. Bliese, and Joseph J. Norton, "Organizational Change and Work Innovation: A Meta-Analysis of 131 North American Field Experiments—1961–1990," working paper (Texas Tech University, 1991).
17. Quoted by Kim Fisher, "Are You Serious About Self-Management?" (paper delivered at the International Conference on Self-Managed Work Teams, Dallas, October 1991).
18. This section is adapted from Sims and Lorenzi, *New Leadership Paradigm.*

Chapter 1

Acknowledgments: We sincerely appreciate the cooperation of Charrette Corporation and especially Lionel Spiro (chairman) in making this chapter possible.

A number of sources were very helpful in preparing this chapter. These include Charles C. Manz and Henry P. Sims, Jr., *SuperLeadership: Leading Others to Lead Themselves* (New York: Berkley, 1990) and Charles C. Manz and Henry P. Sims, Jr., "Leading Workers to Lead Themselves: The External Leadership of Self-Managing Work Teams," *Administrative Science Quarterly* 32 (1987): 106–128. Other helpful sources on the challenges that team work poses for professional employees, managers, executives, and organizations include forthcoming publications by Anne Donnellon: *The Meaning of Team Work*, and "Crossfunctional Teams in Product Development: Accommodating the Organization Structure to the Team Process," *Journal of Product Innovation Management.*

1. Other helpful sources on worker self-management and managing self-managed employees included Edward E. Lawler III, *High Involvement Management* (San Francisco: Jossey-Bass, 1986); J. Richard Hackman, "The Psychology of Self-Management in Organizations," in M. S. Pollack and R. O. Perloff (eds.), *Psychology and Work: Productivity Change and Employment* (Washington, D.C.: American Psychological Association, 1986); and Richard E. Walton, "From Control to Commitment in the Workplace," *Harvard Business Review* 63 (1985): 77–84.
2. For additional information on the challenges of employee self-management and leading self-managing employees, see Fred Luthans and Tim Davis, "Behavioral Self-Management (BSM): The Missing Link in Managerial Effectiveness," *Organizational Dynamics* 8 (1979): 42–60; Richard E. Walton

and Leonard A. Schlesinger, "Do Supervisors Thrive in Participative Work Systems?" *Organizational Dynamics* 8 (1979): 24–39; Charles C. Manz, *Mastering Self-Leadership: Empowering Yourself for Personal Excellence* (Englewood Cliffs, N.J.; Prentice-Hall, 1992); and Charles C. Manz, "Self-Leadership: Toward an Expanded Theory of Self-Influence Processes in Organizations," *Academy of Management Review* 11 (1986): 585–600.

3. For information on methods for analyzing conversations in organizations, see Anne Donnellon, Barbara Gray, and Michael Bougan, "Communication, Meaning and Organizational Action," *Administrative Science Quarterly* 31 (1986): 43–55.

Chapter 2

Acknowledgments: We acknowledge the support of Richard Cherry, who helped to provide access to collect the data for this case and has served as a colleague and adviser over several years. We also acknowledge the exceptional helpfulness and cooperation of management and employees at Fitzgerald.

For readers interested in training, a training case based on the Fitzgerald story, "The Greenfield Case," is available from Organization Design and Development, 2002 Renaissance Blvd., Suite 100, King of Prussia, PA 19406, 213-279-2002.

Parts of this chapter were previously published as Henry P. Sims, Jr., and Charles C. Manz, "Conversations Within Self-Managing Teams," *National Productivity Review* 1 (1982): 261–269, and Charles C. Manz and Henry P. Sims, Jr., "Searching for the Unleader. Organizational Member Views on Leading Self-Managing Groups," *Human Relations* 37 (1984): 409–424. "Searching for the Unleader" provides details and a more quantitative analysis of the findings.

Chapter 3

Acknowledgments: Sincere appreciation is extended to Ted Smith and Fred Zambroski, who were instrumental in providing extensive organizational and operational background information and facilitating the scheduling of interviews that formed the basis for this chapter. We also thank the numerous self-managing team members, team leaders, and design team members of the paper mill for sharing their time and candid comments with us. This chapter is based in part on material previously published: Charles C. Manz and John Newstrom, "Self-Managing Teams in a Paper Mill: Success Factors, Problems, and Lessons Learned," *International Human Resource Management Review* 1 (1990): 43–60.

1. For more information on this issue see C. C. Manz and H. P. Sims, Jr., "Searching for the Unleader: Organizational Member Views on Leading Self-Managed Groups," *Human Relations* 37 (1984): 409–434, and C. C. Manz and H. P. Sims, Jr., "Leading Self-Managed Groups: A Conceptual Analysis of a Paradox," *Economic and Industrial Democracy* 7 (1986): 141–165.

Chapter 4

Acknowledgments: All quotations are taken from interviews conducted with IDS employees during the summer of 1988. We acknowledge the generous cooperation of the IDS people and organization, Bill Scholz, former vice-president; Jim Punch, current vice-president, who was especially instrumental in making the interviews possible; and Becky Smith, who so competently transcribed the interview tapes.

Barry Bateman is currently vice president and partner of Block Petrello, Weisbord, Inc., Plainfield, N.J., a consulting firm specializing in whole system design.

1. The design team discussed whether the compensation system should be revised, but at the time information for this story was collected, this issue had not been resolved. As one member put it, "They are currently meeting on a regular basis to discuss compensation. The task force is made up of team members, management members, human resources people. It's in discussion." Overall, the design team clearly was interested in a "wealth creation" model for the future.
2. The STS approach tends to invest design authority in the design team. Other types of self-managing implementations often leave greater latitude to the teams themselves, once they are underway.
3. This is a summary of the final recommendations. The actual final report was more detailed and complex.
4. At the time data were collected for this study, the change to strategic director had not been implemented, although the current manager team had accepted the recommendation for this change in role. An interesting aspect of this recommendation is that the role of manager had been redesigned by the subordinates of the manager, yet the managers had accepted the redesign.
5. *Wall Street Journal*, August 14, 1991, pp. A1, A4.

Chapter 5

Acknowledgments: This chapter is based in part on material previously published in Charles C. Manz and Harold Angle, "Can Group Self-Management Mean a Loss of Personal Control: Triangulating on a Paradox," *Group and Organization Studies* 11 (1986): 309–334. The original research was partially funded by a grant from the Operations Management Center at the University of Minnesota. The authors are grateful to John Guarino and Rosemarie Orehek for their valuable assistance in data collection. Because of the sensitive nature of the information in this story, the name of the organization is confidential.

1. See, for example, Peter K. Mills, "Self-Management: Its Control and Relationship to Other Organizational Properties," *Academy of Management Review* 8 (1983): 445–453. Peter K. Mills and Barry Z. Posner, "The Relationship Among Self-Supervision, Structure and Technology in Professional Service Organizations," *Academy of Management Journal* 25 (1982): 437–443.
2. See, for example, Albert Bandura, *Social Learning Theory* (Englewood Cliffs, N.J.: Prentice-Hall, 1977), and his "The Self-System in Reciprocal Determinism," *American Psychologist* 33 (1978): 344–358.
3. For more information on the tendency for views espoused by managers to be inconsistent with what they actually do, see Chris Argyris, "Leadership, Learning and the Status Quo," *Organizational Dynamics* 9 (1980): 29–43.
4. For more information on individual employee (as well as team-based self-management and self-leadership), see Charles C. Manz, *Mastering Self-Leadership: Empowering Yourself for Personal Excellence* (Englewood Cliffs, N.J.: Prentice-Hall, 1992), and Charles C. Manz and Henry P. Sims, Jr., *Super-Leadership: Leading Others to Lead Themselves* (New York: Berkley, 1990).

Chapter 6

Acknowledgments: A number of sources were especially helpful in providing background material for this chapter. The most important sources of all were the W. L. Gore associates who generously shared their time and viewpoints about the company. We especially appreciate the assistance of Anita McBride, who spent hours with us and provided many resources, including internal documents and videotapes.

1. A number of published sources are available for obtaining more information on Gore, including the following: S. W. Angrist, "Classless Capitalists," *Forbes*, May 9, 1983, pp. 123–124; J. Hoerr, "A Company Where Every-

body Is the Boss," *Business Week*, April 15, 1985, p. 98; K. Price, "Firm Thrives Without Boss," *AZ Republic*, February 2, 1986; B. G. Posner, "The First Day on the Job," *Inc.* (June 1986): 73–75; L. Rhodes, "The Un-manager," *Inc.* (August 1982): 34; J. Simmons, "People Managing Themselves: Un-management at W. L. Gore Inc.," *Journal for Quality and Participation* (December 1987): 14–19; A. Ward, "An All-Weather Idea," *New York Times Magazine*, November 10, 1985; "Wilbert L. Gore," *Industry Week*, October 17, 1983, pp. 48–49.

2. Gore's ASOP is similar legally to an ESOP (employee stock option plan). Gore simply does not use the word "employee" in any of its documentation.

Chapter 7

Acknowledgments: We thank the staff at Texas Instruments Malaysia, especially Jerry Lee, Mohd Azmi Abdullah, A. Subramaniam, and Gene Carlone.

1. Peter F. Drucker, "The Responsible Worker," in his *Management: Task, Responsibilities, Practices.* Allied Publishers Private Limited, 1975, India.
2. For more on this topic, see Henry P. Sims, Jr., and James W. Dean, "Beyond Quality Circles: Evolution into Self-Managing Teams," *Personnel* (January 1985): 25–32.

Chapter 8

Acknowledgments: Most of the quotations in this chapter are from on-site interviews conducted from 1990 to 1992. We are especially thankful to Dennis Bakke, who facilitated the project, and to the special cooperation of AES employees. Other material is excerpted from AES's June 1991 prospectus and the 1991 annual report.

1. Edward E. Lawler III, *High Involvement Management* (San Francisco: Jossey-Bass, 1986); Charles C. Manz and Henry P. Sims, Jr., *SuperLeadership: Leading Others to Lead Themselves* (New York: Berkley, 1990).

Chapter 9

1. Kim Fisher, "The Role of the Manager in Self-Directed Work Teams," (presentation at the 1991 International SMWT Conference, Dallas, October 14, 1991).

2. In Charles C. Manz and Henry P. Sims, Jr., *SuperLeadership: Leading Others to Lead Themselves* (New York: Berkley, 1990), we detail how leaders can lead others to lead themselves.

3. See Charles C. Manz, *Mastering Self-Leadership: Empowering Yourself for Personal Excellence* (Englewood Cliffs, N.J.: Prentice-Hall, 1992), for a description of how to teach self-leadership skills.

4. For example, see R. E. Walton, "The Diffusion of New Work Structures: Explaining Why Success Didn't Take," *Organizational Dynamics* (Winter 1975): 3–22.

5. For an extensive discussion of this point, see H. P. Sims, Jr., and James W. Dean, "Beyond Quality Circles: Evolution into Self-Managing Teams," *Personnel*, January 1985, pp. 25–32.

6. Brian Dumaine, "Who Needs a Boss?" *Fortune*, May 7, 1990, pp. 52–60; and John Horr, "The Payoff from Teamwork," *Business Week*, July 10, 1989, pp. 56–62.

7. See Tom Peters, "Excellence in the Public Sector," PBS, 1990.

8. For a training case that addresses this issue, see "The Greenfield Case," available from Organizational Design and Development, 2002 Renaissance Blvd., Suite 100, King of Prussia, PA 19406.

9. Manz and Sims, *SuperLeadership*, pp. xv–xvi.

10. For more information on what happens when top leaders step down, see Jeffrey Sonnenfeld, *The Hero's Farewell: What Happens When CEOs Retire* (New York: Oxford University Press, 1988).

11. For more on self-leadership, see Manz, *Mastering Self-Leadership*.

Index